U.S. NAVY
SEALS
IN ACTION

HANS HALBERSTADT

BARNES
&NOBLE
BOOKS
NEW YORK

For my brother Erik

First published in 1995 by MBI Publishing Company
Galtier Plaza, Suite 200, 380 Jackson Street,
St. Paul, MN 55101-3885 USA

This edition published by Barnes & Noble, Inc.,
by arrangement with MBI Publishing Company

2001 Barnes & Noble Books

M 10 9 8 7 6 5 4 3 2 1

ISBN 0-7607-2769-4

© Hans Halberstadt, 1995

The information in this book is true and complete to the best of our
knowledge. All recommendations are made without any guarantee
on the part of the author or Publisher, who also disclaim any
liability incurred in connection with the use of this data or specific
details.
We recognize that some words, model names and designations, for
example, mentioned herein are the property of the trademark
holder. We use them for identification purposes only. This is not an
official publication.

Library of Congress Cataloging-in-Publication Data Available

On the front cover: This is something you would never see: a U.S.
Navy SEAL standing out in the open during the daytime. This SEAL
poses for the camera in his jungle attire and holds a squad
automatic weapon (SAW). *Robert Genat/Arms Communications*

On the frontispiece: A SEAL is silhouetted while poised for action.
Hans Halberstadt

On the title page: A boatload of trouble is headed your way. A team
of SEALs moves across the water in an inflatable.
Robert Genat/Zone Five photo

On the back cover: A pair of SEALs (they move in teams of at least
two men) make a landing and are ready to carry out their mission.
Hans Halberstadt

Printed in Hong Kong

Contents

Acknowledgments

Many thanks to Rear Admiral Ray Smith for his virtually unique support of enlightened public affairs during his tenure as Commander, US Navy Special Warfare Command (SPECWARCOM).

Thanks also to LCDR John Brinley, former Public Affairs Officer for SPECWARCOM, for holding the door open while a few of us peeked inside.

A sincere salute to the many current active-duty and Reserve SEALs and Special Boat Squadron crew who provided support. In any other book I would list them by name—but not for this one. Conflict resolution, US Navy SEAL-style, can be hazardous to your health and most SEALs like to keep a low profile. Some, though, understand that the taxpaying American public needs to know what they're buying and that books like this one can help people understand the community without putting anybody at risk... or, at least no more risk than they are already.

But I can publicly salute two career SEALs who provided me with tremendous insights to real-world Naval Special Warfare operations, Capt. Bob Gormley and Commander Gary Stubblefield. Capt. Gormley's combat experience started along the rivers and canals of the Mekong Delta and he later commanded the renowned SEAL Team SIX, relieving its legendary (and much-beloved, too) inventor Capt. Dick Marcinko.

Commander Gary Stubblefield (former commander of SEAL Team THREE, SEAL platoon leader in Viet Nam, commander of NAVSPECWAR Task Unit *Pacific* during Operation Ernest Will in the Persian Gulf, and commander of Special Boat Squadron *ONE*) is undoubtedly the most articulate, informed, opinionated—and respected—advocate for the Naval Special Warfare community. Gary, unlike so many in NSW today, is an operator with "combat time" in Southeast Asia, Central America, and the Persian Gulf, with an "operator's" perspective toward weapons, tactics, training, and doctrine. Unlike so many in the community today, Gary has actually been shot at. His participation on this book provides a depth and breadth not available elsewhere.

Finally, thanks to Robert and Robin Genat—friends and colleagues with their own book on the SEAL community—for their generous contributions to a competing project.

Preface

by Cdr. Gary Stubblefield, USN (ret), former commander of SEAL Team THREE

Writing about SEALs is a tough job. There is an inherent reticence by the Naval Special Warfare community and its men to provide meaningful information to any reporter or author—and for good reason. Any SEAL who stays around for more than one hitch is bound to encounter the stereotypical author looking for a sensational story or an "exposé" of this unique and elite community and its secrets. Couple that with a continual mind-set that everything a SEAL does has to be kept from any *potential* enemy, and the result is an organization that shuns any sort of media attention.

I remember one reporter from the *Navy Times* who gained access to the SEALs through a three-star admiral. We were directed to put forth a positive effort to give this individual a first-ever opportunity to live with us, eat with us, and watch us for ten days. He took pictures, recorded training data, and listened to the men intently. Three months later when the article came out, it was short of facts, long on sensational anecdotes lifted from previous books and articles. When I confronted the reporter he said that what he wrote sold better than what we told him. That, sadly, is a typical attitude.

As a result, locating accurate information on SEAL units is next to impossible for most readers interested in what we do. No writers get to go to the field with us on actual missions because the reporter would have to be a SEAL just to keep up. What we do in the real world, as a result, has traditionally been invisible. For these reasons, most of what you see in print elsewhere has either been sensational or has focused on the one area of Naval Special Warfare where members of the news media are sometimes permitted, the training course at Coronado called BUD/S.

However, if a writer or photographer is stubborn enough, persistent enough, it is possible to gradually collect enough information, stories, and photographs to describe what it is like to be a Navy SEAL.

Hans has done just that. He first became friends with some of us who have been taught to distrust anyone with a pen or camera. Once he gained our trust and proved he wasn't out to present a sensational exposé, he was able to learn what equipment a SEAL carries, what a SEAL does, and most importantly, what makes a SEAL tick. He has seen the strengths and recognized some of the weaknesses; he has focused on the strengths—with just a little humor to make it interesting. He has described a few problems we have in the NSW community without taking them out of context or making them the target of the book. For these reasons, this book is a more accurate portrait than many others that have attempted to tell our story.

I hope the readers of this book recognize that, as taxpayers, they are getting their money's worth. There are no more dedicated, better trained men in any branch of the military ready to defend our great nation than those in the US Navy SEALs.

Chapter One

Laying on
the Mission
US Navy SEALs Today

The organization known today as the US Navy SEALs is quite rightly considered among the premiere fighting forces in the world, along with the "Green Berets," Russian Spetznaz, British Special Air Service (SAS), most of the Israeli army, and the French Foreign Legion. These small congregations of fighting men are sometimes called "commandos," sometimes called the most elite of combat soldiers; both are true—and both parts of the legend are misleading. Members of the SEAL community are mortals; they bleed and hurt and die. They aren't, as some seem to think, immortal or infallible. One of the interesting parts of the story of this fabled crew is just how often SEAL missions have turned into bloody disasters. While the courage of individual SEALs is without question, the wisdom of some recent operations has been dubious. It makes the story even more interesting.

Today's SEALs are the descendants of a long line of US Navy, British, and Italian combat swimmers. The SEAL mission has evolved over the years, the equipment has changed, and the tactics and strategy for employing SEALs has been gradually modified by the time and tide of world events. Fifty years ago, during World War II, the mission was to chart invasion beaches and clear obstacles before amphibious assaults. Those early "frogmen" were strictly subordinate to a local task force commander, tasked with a very limited mission that didn't extend past the high water mark. Today's SEALs still have that mission—plus many others. Not only has the mission expanded, the chain of command has shifted, too; the task force commander may wear

SEALs have a reputation as being among the most elite combatants in anybody's armed forces. The reputation is earned, in part, because the SEAL mission includes some of the most dangerous, difficult procedures asked of any soldier or sailor—particularly the kind of sub-surface swim this combat swimmer from SEAL Team Five is prepared to do. Foto Consortium

Right: Rear Admiral Ray Smith likes to say that SEALs are "quiet professionals," and they try to be especially quiet at moments like this. After a long transit from a submarine aboard a Swimmer Delivery Vehicle (SDV) comes one of the dangerous and critical moments of a mission, the "insertion" phase when the SEALs leave the protection of the water for the uncertain fates and fortunes of the shore.

SEALs, like every other component of the armed forces of the United States, uses human beings to project power. That power is designed to make things happen in ways favorable to the interests of the American people. The huge weight of that responsibility ultimately trickles down the chain of command to people like these two men, stepping into the tremendously dangerous waters of Viet Nam's Rung Sat Special Zone. Far better than American conventional force units, the Navy's SEALs and the Army's Special Forces made a tremendous positive difference in Viet Nam, inventing the new American military art called "special operations." U.S. Navy

a star or two but the SEAL team embarked on his ships often get their orders from other authorities.

Many of these changes are the result of a major overhaul of the American armed forces during the middle of the 1980s. After the debacle in the Iranian desert, wholesale changes were demanded by Congress in the Goldwater–Nichols act of 1984. Among other things, this act mandated that Naval Special Warfare would be a "flag" rank component of the Special Operations Command.

SEALs today are just one part of a collection of extremely well-trained, generously equipped, and (for their small size) lavishly funded American military organizations that collectively are known as the Joint Special Operations

Command (JSOC, pronounced "jay-sock"). Serving alongside the SEALs—and dominating JSOC—are the Army's legendary "Green Berets" and Rangers; the Army also contributes an aviation unit to the team, Task Force 160, the Nightstalkers. The Air Force is part of the JSOC team; its Special Operations Wing provides C-130 Spectre gunships and Pave Hawk and Pave Low helicopters to support the missions. The days when the Army, Navy, Air Force, and Marine Corps operated independently, with their own missions, men, radio frequencies, logistics train, and command structures, are long gone.

Instead, since the bloody, embarrassing lessons of the Iranian hostage rescue mission and the invasion of Grenada during the mid-1980s, special operations units like the SEALs and the Green Berets provide mutual support and interlocking fields of fire. In the community it is a policy called "joint-

Right: Lt. JG William Bishop, back aboard a Navy landing craft after a bad day in the boonies, was one of the pioneers in the Naval Special Warfare back in 1967 when this shot was made. Bishop, a member of SEAL Team ONE, had to help invent ways to conduct operations in a place the Navy didn't really want to be, a mission the Navy was essentially ordered to perform. Special operators in all the services are accustomed to being resented in subtle ways—besides being given the nastiest missions possible. U.S. Navy

Left: SEALs are rather notorious for dispensing with the usual starch and polish demanded by conventional forces. This team member sports a full, ragged beard and wears a triangular bandage ("drive-on rag" in the vernacular) instead of a hat. Appearance is only one part of the SEAL community's way to remind the conventional Navy that SEALs sometimes play an unconventional game with unconventional rules. U.S. Navy

Today's SEALs have their origins with the Underwater Demolition Teams (UDTs), begun during World War II and incorporated into the SEAL teams in 1982. These UDT swimmers are rehearsing one of their many non-combat collateral duties, in this case providing rescue swimmer services for an Apollo capsule in the Pacific Ocean. U.S. Navy

ness," and the SEALs are the dampest guys in the joint. It is a sometimes awkward, contentious, occasionally petty kind of relationship where competition for missions, support, influence, and funding push and pull at individuals and com-

munities. Right now some SEALs fret that the Army's Green Berets and Rangers—who heavily outnumber the SEALs—have diverted the traditional mission of Naval Special Warfare from missions in and around the water to something much drier, much more like the Army's role.

Brazilian and American special operators dash to board a SH-3 Sea King helicopter during a joint training exercise at Roosevelt Roads, Puerto Rico. SEALs work closely with their counterparts in many of the world's armed forces. U.S. Navy

Home port for all US Navy special ops is a small compound on the sunny strand at Coronado, California. Here, behind the barbed wire and just a pitch and a putt from the historic and elegant Hotel Del Coronado, the admiral in command of US Naval Special Warfare Command (SPECWARCOM) and his staff plan for SEAL missions around the globe, develop policy

and training procedures, and keep a weather eye on international events. This is the command post for SEAL teams TWO, FOUR, and EIGHT (based in Little Creek, Virginia) and ONE, THREE, and FIVE (based alongside SPECWARCOM and buds at Coronado) as well as for all forward-deployed units and elements serving with the fleet and overseas.

In this same pleasant spot, alongside the bevies of tourists frolicking on the beach, apprentice SEALs endure the most brutal, challenging, and dangerous training program in the US armed forces, the Basic Underwater Demolition/SEAL (BUD/S) course. It is a program that quickly separates the weak (in mind and body both) from the strong—a course

Above: SEALs and a very few other members of the U.S. armed forces are warriors in ways quite unlike those in the rest of the military. They share many of the skills, traditions, and techniques used by the Indian warrior tribes of 200 years ago. No one joins this little tribe without enduring an ordeal that very few can complete, then participates in a community with extremely demanding missions and traditions.

Left: SEALs have many kinds of missions, one of which involves slow, stealthy movement deep into enemy territory. In an age of tremendous technical sophistication, there are times when there is no substitute for having people on the ground, ready and able to report on conditions, designate targets, or to execute attacks.

where more than half the students typically fail, and where serious injuries are commonplace. Even the Army's "Green Berets," who endure a similar six-month program, often candidly admit that BUD/S is the most physically challenging qualification program in the armed services.

SPECWARCOM is built around "fleets" of forces, one on the East Coast and one on the West. Naval Special Warfare Group *TWO* is headquartered in Little Creek, Virginia, and faces the vast Atlantic Ocean and all the potential battlegrounds and beaches from the Baltic to Cape Horn. Naval Special Warfare Group *ONE*, based in Coronado, is responsible for operations from the US Pacific coast around the globe to Africa's east coast.

Each Group has two *major* kinds of forces, one whose missions are above the surface, the other below. Each

Above: Like Indian warriors, SEALs use standard tactics for mutual support. This fire team (half a squad—four men) adopt a circular formation. Each man has a sector of responsibility; they will avoid firing it at all possible.

Left: SEAL recon missions involve a lot of watching and very little shooting. In fact, if you have to shoot your weapon on a recon you've probably blundered. The ideal recon involves slipping into your objective area unnoticed, collecting information, and getting back out again without leaving a trace.

Group commands three SEAL teams, a SEAL Delivery Vehicle (SDV) team, and a Special Boat Squadron staff commanding two Special Boat Units. This elevation of the Boat Units to major command status is something new, and important. The men in most of the boats aren't SEALs and are drawn from the surface Navy, but these boat units do more than just deliver the combat swimmers to the surf zone—they have a heavy combat capability on their own, with a rich heritage of combat experience during Viet Nam and later. Serving alongside both the boat drivers and the combat swimmers are many supporting players who develop new kinds of equip-

ment, and operate the exotic little SEAL submarine called the SDV (Mk VIII SEAL Delivery Vehicle), and all the "headquarters pukes" and "staff weenies" who plan, plot, and scheme to keep the whole organization agile and strong, able to accept unconventional missions with unconventional speed and effectiveness.

The SEAL Teams

While the teams are organized, supported, and trained by SPECWARCOM, they become assets of a theater commander once they are deployed.

Unlike conventional military forces, the SEAL teams' basic weapons aren't bought but are "manufactured" at Coronado; the basic weapon is what people in the community call the "Mark One, Mod Zero SEAL." That weapon is a human being—a young or middle-aged man, superficially the same as many others in the fleet or in the armed services, but with some major differences. Each SEAL is the product of an intense distillation process called BUD/S, a six-month ordeal that filters out all but men with a very unusual combination of physical, emotional, and intellectual strength. Each graduate of the program has the characteristics of Olympic athletes: a tolerance for pain, a gift of

Above and next page: In the grand Indian tradition, SEALs learn to become virtually invisible—a low-tech version of the Stealth fighter.

strength, speed, and agility. But SEALs must have other abilities not required of athletes: judgment, an excellent memory, a detailed knowledge of hundreds of weapons, systems, procedures, policies.

five of these are support and logistics people from the surface fleet: parachute riggers, intel specialists, armorers, electronic technicians, personnel clerks—all necessary to keep the SEALs and the Special Boat Squadrons operating. Another forty provide training and command and control support functions for the platoons. The sharp end of each team, the fighting part, are the ten *platoons* of SEALs who get the tactical assignments. These platoons are each composed of two *squads* of eight men each; the platoon commander (typically a lieutenant) will command one of the squads while the platoon executive officer (always called the 2IC—"Second in Command") will command the other. Each of these squads are further subdivided into two *fire teams* of four SEALs each.

Special Boat Squadrons

Although the boats don't get the glory of the SEALs, they are equal on the organization chart, and in real life, too. That translates to lavish funding for things like the new 170ft Patrol Coastal ship, a new system for keeping experienced people within the special ops community, and a growing dependency on the capabilities of the squadrons. This development is taking SPECWARCOM off on a rather new course—one that many SEALs think is inappropriate to the traditional stealthy, close inshore mission. But this new vessel is designed as both a coastal patrol craft and as a launch platform for SEAL missions, complete with many features intended expressly for the teams. It is the first ship dedicated to the needs of this community. More about the PC later.

There are changes for the crews of the Special Boat Squadrons, too; until recently the "boat drivers" were conventional sailors right out of the surface fleet on two-year tours. They pulled a hitch in the little rigid-hull inflatable boats (officially designated RIBs) and the speedy "cigarette boats" and then returned to billets aboard frigates, cruisers, and carriers. Now the Special Boat Squadrons will have their own dedicated professionals with a new Naval career specialty, *Combat Craft Crewman*. These crews will be, like the SEALs themselves, strictly volunteers. They will become an integral,

Teams ONE, THREE and FIVE are all based at Coronado; Teams TWO, FOUR and EIGHT work out of Little Creek. Each team is staffed by about 225 men, only 160 of whom are actually members of the platoons; twenty-

A rifleman from SEAL Team Three waits for the party to begin. The weapon is a CAR (Colt Automatic Rifle)–15, a compact version of the same M-16 that is the standard personal weapon throughout the US armed forces.

permanent part of the Naval Special Warfare community. This is an important change.

A Dehydrated History of Combat Swimmers

Americans like to begin their history lessons with their national participation in the topic, as if nothing happened until their tried it. Most American discussions of SEAL history begin with 1943 and the invasion of Tarawa—*Terrible Tarawa* it has always been to the Marines, with reason. That disastrous amphibious assault was conducted without a beach survey; the assault craft delivering the Marines to the beach were halted half a mile offshore. The Marines debarked, tried to wade ashore, and were slaughtered before they could even hit the beach. The cost was so high that the Navy quickly began a combat swimmer program that ultimately became the Underwater Demolition Teams (UDT) and much later the SEALs.

Modern combat swim programs began during World War II all right, but not because of any innovative

thinking of the US Navy, who adopted the idea quite late. It was the Italians (who have received very little credit for anything during World War II) who really invented and developed and inspired the idea of what used to be called "frogmen" back in 1935.

SEALs are part of the "special operations" community, a consortium of Army, Air Force, and Navy units designed and built to provide quick response to several kinds of emergencies: hostage seizures, terrorist attacks, rescues. Here US Air Force MH-53J "Pave Low" helicopters, the battlefield taxi of choice, pull over to the curb while a contingent of SEALs swarm aboard. Rick Mullen/Foto Consortium

"Hmmmm... those girls are really cute." While SEALs have access to the latest in image intensification technology, including extreme low-light intensifiers, thermal imaging viewers, along with laser range finders and target designators, the "Mk One Eyeball" remains the most reliable—even if it is sometimes distracted a bit.

Right: A member of SEAL Team Three with the tools of his trade. The whip antenna identifies him as a radio operator ("RTO," for Radio-Telephone Operator); the RTO is a prime target for any enemy sniper in range because of his critical role as the squad's link to the rest of the world. The squad will not set foot on hostile shores without a "fire support" plan—the services of jet fighters, attack helicopters, artillery, or naval gunfire support, all on call when the RTO keys the handset switch. His other weapon is a CAR-15 with M203 40mm grenade launcher attached.

Italian Pollywogs Strike the First Blow

The concept was hatched in October, 1935, by two young Italian Navy officers, sub-lieutenants Toschi and Tesei. Their proposal was for a manned long-range torpedo, controlled by a crew of two swimmers. The 1930s were an innovative time for the Italian military, and the concept was blessed by Admiral Cavagnari. An experimental version of the design was built and tested in La Spezia harbor during December of 1936. The test was successful enough that a full development program, called Department H, was authorized.

The weapon was 22ft long and 21in in diameter; propulsion was provided by electric batteries and motors powering twin counter-rotating propellers. Since the crew had to ride the weapon astride, top speed was limited to just three knots to keep them from being washed away. It wallowed like a pig—so that's what the crews

called it. A 500 pound (lb) warhead was up front in the usual spot, but instead of conventional torpedo impact or magnetic influence fusing, this one was designed to be removed from the torpedo by the crew and attached to the hull of the target ship below the keel.

The crew had to find their target in the dark, make an undetected approach and then maneuver the "pig" below the keel of the vessel. Then the ballast tanks were emptied, raising the torpedo into contact with the keel. The divers then attached clamps and cables to the bilge keels of the target ship. The warhead, released from the torpedo, was then attached to the cable where it hung directly below the vulnerable keel. The fuses were set for two and a half hours—and the crew then hopped back

harbor turned out to be empty of targets for the new weapons. One of the two subs was attacked on the return voyage and Lt. Cdr. Toschi, along with the rest of the crew, was captured—without the British still knowing anything about the weapon or the project.

SEALs may be capable individuals but on operations they never do anything alone. The basic element for any operation begins with a "swim pair," two SEALs who provide mutual support for each other. In the water they will even be connected with a 6ft line; ashore they will be connected with a fifty-year tradition. No matter how bad things get, one SEAL will not abandon another on an operation, even in death.

aboard their faithful steed and beat a not-too-hasty retreat at three knots.

By August 1940, with World War II well under way, the submersible weapon and its pollywog crew was ready for trial by fire. Three of the weapons were installed on the deck of the Italian submarine *Iride*; British patrol aircraft found the sub out in the Mediterranean, though, before the torpedoes could be launched and the sub was sent to the bottom. A month later two other Italian subs tried again, both with two torpedoes; this mission also aborted when Alexandria

The Italians launched several more abortive attacks in 1941. Lt. Cdr. Tesei, the other inventor of the weapon, was also captured and some of the crew were killed. Now the Brits were aware of the idea and the fleet was warned to expect attacks from unconventional weapons.

Volunteers were recruited for a program called the Under Water Working Parties—shallow water divers to combat human torpedoes, remove limpet mines, recover weapons and bodies from downed aircraft in the water, and clear ship propeller and condenser inlets at sea. Their only breathing apparatus were the simple oxygen sets designed to allow submarine crews to ascend to the surface; they were dangerous, but available, so they were used. These British divers soon had work to do; they started finding limpet mines on the hulls of merchant ships after port calls in neutral Spain.

The human torpedoes finally scored on 19 September 1941 when three of the crews attacked shipping targets in Gibraltar's harbor. One got past the anti-

Log PT ("physical training") is exhausting, the worst part of the physical conditioning program at Coronado for many students. The activity occurs right on the beach with all the San Diego-area tourists and sunbathers. Gary L. Kieffer/Foto Consortium

submarine net and executed a text book attack on the merchant ship *Denbydale.* All three crews escaped to nearby Spanish territory where they were flown back to Italy—and heroes' receptions.

Two months later the Italians attacked again, this time against bigger game. Count Luigi de la Pene and his assistant attacked the British battleship *Valiant* in Alexandria harbor. Although unable to attach the warhead as designed, de la Pene scuttled the torpedo below the keel and both crewmen were captured by the ship's crew while trying to escape... and locked in the brig, right above the spot where the warhead was due to explode. With five minutes left, Count de la Pene sent a message to the *Valiant's* captain, warning of the imminent blast. The crew of the ship—and both Italian prisoners—were quickly brought on deck before the warhead detonated. Nobody was injured but the ship was severely damaged. Then a blast rocked another battle-

ship, the Queen Elizabeth, and a naval tanker. All of the crewmen were captured. Later, after the Italians capitulated to the allies, the British Navy captain of the *Valiant* participated in a Italian ceremony honoring Count de la Pene for his valor in the attack on the his own vessel.

British

British reaction was swift, innovative, and effective. Combat swimmers were quickly recruited and trained; equipment, missions, and tactics developed to counter the enemy threat. Soon, British frogmen began a program of inspecting the hulls of ships for mines. Often, this had to be done strictly by touch. The program paid off; enemy frogmen were captured and killed. One British frogman, the legendary Lt. "Bill" Bailey, fought and killed an Italian with his dive knife in an encounter below the surface of Gibraltar harbor during 1942.

The British Navy started another, related program that same year, a super-secret unit called Combined Operations Pilotage Parties (COPP). The COPP concept was a beach recon outfit, equipped with kayaks, tasked with surveying potential sites for amphibious assaults. The unit sent four teams in before the landings in Sicily.

US Navy Scouts and Raiders

By the time the US Navy got serious about using combat swimmers, the war was half over. But the American program was cobbled together, men recruited, trained, and launched into combat. The mission for American frogmen was quite different than for the British or Italians; instead of offensive ship-attack or defense missions, USN swimmers were tasked primarily with supporting amphibious landings. The problem for American forces in 1943 was getting the landing force safely across the beach in strength—and that required knowing a great deal about the beach before the assault was planned or launched.

In some ways, that program fifty years ago wasn't all that different from what apprentice SEALs endure today: too much running, too much PT (physical training), too much swimming, too much familiarity with explosives, small arms, and unarmed combat for any but the most durable man. If any of the recruits expected their stay in sunny Florida to be

Real-world missions for SEALs are so challenging that the BUD/S program is designed to replicate that stress as much as possible in a peacetime training environment. Far more than other training, BUD/S is downright dangerous; broken bones are common, injuries universal. This student won't get any sympathy from the instructors if he's cut from the wire, abraded from the ground, or if his feet are bleeding from all the running students do every day. It is all part of the program. U.S. Navy

an enjoyable respite from duties with the fleet, they soon had their attitudes adjusted. The instructors at Ft. Pierce pushed their tadpoles through drill after drill, stress after stress.

The students learned to swim long distances, map beaches, and, later, use explosives to clear obstacles. Their equipment was nearly non-existent: no fins, no wet suits (except the overalls they sometimes used as protection against rock and coral), no breathing apparatus. They were issued a plastic slate and a grease pencil, though, and a lead-line to measure depth. And, as it turned out, this was enough.

BUD/S training combines stress with real-world worst-case skills to filter out all but the most resolute. The staff of BUD/S, themselves all victims of the program, never know for sure who will survive and who will fail. Gary Kieffer/Foto Consortium

The Army began in early 1943 to experiment with techniques for blowing up the same kinds of steel and concrete obstacles used by Japanese and German forces. These tests went on alongside the training for the combat swimmers at Ft. Pierce, although the programs were originally independent. But it didn't take long for the Navy to say, "hey, that's *our* job!" And then beach clearance became part of the Navy mission, too.

Chief of Naval Operations (CNO) Ernest King authorized a revised program for naval combat swimmers on 6 June 1943, a unit christened the Naval Demolition Unit. Besides providing hydrographic surveys for amphibious task force commanders, this new creation was intended to clear lanes through anti-invasion obstacles placed by enemy defenders—and, at that time, the primary defenders were expected to be German.

Two kinds of combat swimmer units developed during this time. The first, with a focus on the invasion of continental Europe, were thirteen-man Naval Combat Demolition Units. In the Pacific much larger Underwater Demolition Teams included ninety-six officers and men.

The UDTs got their first taste of fire just two months after bloody Tarawa, on the last day of January 1944, at a place called Kwajalein. Two UDTs participated, Team ONE assigned to the US Army's 7th Division, Team TWO supporting the Marine 4th Division. Both conducted nighttime recons of selected beaches and both confirmed the suitability for use by assault boats. Team ONE was further tasked with two risky daylight surveys and provided critical data about enemy emplacements and potential hazards from portions of the coral reef just offshore.

Another invasion beckoned just three weeks later, this time the little island of Eniwetok. Saipan followed in June, then Guam, and then Peleliu. As the spearheads pushed deeper into the empire of Imperial Japan, combat swimmers from the UDTs were all the way out front at one beachhead after another.

Normandy

Only one year after the conception of the infant organization, Navy combat swimmers led the charge into Nazi Europe on the 6th of June, 1944. The invasion beaches along

A SEALs Glossary

Here are some terms, acronyms, abbreviations, and jargon used by the SEALs. You'll find these terms and abbreviations used throughout this book.

ARG: Amphibious Ready Group
AT-4: Anti-armor rocket launchers
Attack Board (or Compass Board): A basic tool for navigating during sub-surface combat swims; a simple board with a compass, depth gauge, and watch attached
BDU: Battle Dress Uniform
BUD/S: Basic Underwater Demolition/SEAL, SEAL training course operated at Corondo, just outside San Diego, California.
C4: Flexible plastic explosives used in numerous applications
CAR-15: A compact version of the standard M16 rifle
CATF: Commander, Amphibious Task Force
CNO: Chief of Naval Operations
COPP: Combined Operations Pilotage Parties, a British Navy program in World War II
CRRC: Combat Rubber Raiding Craft
CS: Tear gas
CSAR: Combat Search and Rescue
DPV: Desert Patrol Vehicle
Det Cord: Detonating cord, fuse-like cord used to trigger explosions, often near-simultaneous explosions at various locations
Draeger Mk V: Underwater air supply equipment
E&E: Escape and evasion plan
GPS: Global Positioning System
H&K MP-5: Heckler & Koch MP-5 machine gun
HE: High explosive
HAHO: A high altitude jump, high altitude parachute opening
HALO: A high altitude jump, low altitude parachute opening
HSB: High Speed Boat
JSOC (pronounced "jay-sock"): Joint Special Operations Command
LBE: Load-Bearing Equipment
LSSC: Light SEAL Support Craft
Light Sticks: Flexible plastic tubes containing chemicals that, when mixed, illuminate and act as lights or beacons
Limpet Mine: An explosive device made to be carried on a swimmer's back, then detached and attached to a vessel's hull
M-14: A rifle employed by the SEALs
M-18 Claymore: An explosive device employed by the SEALs; it is basically a mine fired electrically with an electric blasting cap
M-60 E3: A machine gun that's a scaled-down version of the M-60 gun
M-67: A "baseball" grenade; an anti-personnel weapon
M-203: A single-shot, 40mm weapon
Mk 138 Satchel Charge: A canvas bag full of explosives
MATC: A fast river support craft used by SEAL platoons
MRE: Meal, Ready to Eat
MSSC: Medium SEAL Support Craft
NSW: NAVSPECWAR, or Naval Special Warfare
NVG: Night Vision Goggles
PBL: Patrol Boat Light
PC: Patrol Coastal ship or boat
PT: Physical training
RIB: Rigid Inflatable Boat
SAS: Britain's Special Air Service
SDV: SEAL Delivery Vehicle
SOC: Special Operations Command
SOP: Standard Operating Procedure
Spec Ops: Special Operations
Special Boat Squadrons: Naval boat operators and crews that work in concert with SEALs on missions
SPECWARCOM: US Naval Special Warfare Command
UDT: Underwater Demolition Team, a forerunner to SEALs

Next page top: BUD/S emphasizes teamwork and boat crews live or die together, as a unit. From the beginning, boat crews are pushed to compete with each other. The only prize for being first is a little rest, then the pressure begins again.

Next page bottom: "Hell Week" at BUD/S puts students through a kind of living hell that is normally prohibited by regulation elsewhere in the armed forces. It lasts for five and a half days—of constant activity and stress, with no more than a few minutes sleep each day. By day three the students will, if they are still around, begin to hallucinate. Gary Kieffer/Foto Consortium

So you want to be a SEAL? Try this at home until your muscles catch fire, then hold the position for another 10 seconds, then recover. Then you move on to a different kind of torture.

the Normandy coast had been well and skillfully studded with numerous steel and concrete obstacles; 175 members of gap-assault teams, working with US Army combat engineers, stepped off AMTRACs and landing craft at 0633 hours, into the frigid surf, and went to work.

With satchel charges and detonating cord, under constant fire from machine guns, mortars, rifles, and

artillery, they positioned their charges, tied them together with det cord, and lit the fuses. It took five hours, but by noon five lanes had been opened through the defenses for tanks, half-tracks, scout cars, and all the fighting vehicles that would help seize the toe-hold on Nazi Europe. By the end of the day over half the combat swimmers were dead, wounded, or missing. But the assault poured across the beach, into France, one division after another all day; it was, in military terms, a small price for the success of such a critical operation.

The history of Naval Special Warfare during the fifty-plus years since Normandy is an epic tale—well told by many history books, some listed in the appendix—and far too rich and varied to fit in this volume. But one brittle little encounter after another, seldom involving more than a very few men, has gradually modified the US Navy's doctrine, weapons, training, equipment, tactics, and emphasis on combat swim missions and maritime unconventional warfare. Korea, Viet Nam, Grenada, Panama, and the Persian Gulf have each had an influence on the men and the missions of the Navy's special ops community. This book is primarily a portrait of NSW during the 1990s. Another book in ten or twenty years will doubtless show different weapons, different radios, and the boats may be quite unlike what you see here. The men, though, will not be much different than those you see here, and today's SEALs aren't really much different than those of half a century ago, back in the waters off the Normandy coast or the Japanese-held island beaches across the Pacific. The ultimate weapon in the arsenal of the US armed forces has been and will be its people and their warrior spirit. That is not likely to change.

That cargo net is 60ft high. That might not seem like much until you get up there a ways, with the things squirming under foot. The idea is to get up and over in a minimum amount of time—and around the whole obstacle course as fast as you can. Your time for the course must improve if you expect to stay at BUD/S, a place where "good enough" never is.

Previous pages top left: Here is somebody right at the edge of his personal limit—or so he thinks. He is about to fail, and when he does the other seven guys on the boat crew will have to hold up his portion in addition to their own. That mental pressure, very much on the student's mind right now, drives people to accomplish things they would otherwise never attempt. That, too, is part of the program at BUD/S—the development of a "can-do-no-matter-what" attitude that carries over to life in the teams.

Previous pages top right: Pull-ups begin from a full hanging position. Only at the command of the PT leader will the students begin.

Previous pages bottom: As bad as every day at BUD/S may seem, every student participates as a volunteer. If you just can't go on another minute, that's fine with the instructors. Relief is instantly available by walking to the bell out by the "grinder" and ringing it three times—and you are out of there, buddy. About half of every BUD/S class will quit or be failed; in one class, not a single student graduated.

Previous page: Push-ups are part of the daily routine. Upper body strength is a requirement for success at BUD/S and in the teams. That's because those muscles are required for steering a MC-1 parachute, paddling a CRRC, fast-roping from a helicopter, or garroting a sentry out in the real world.

How bad do you want it? The mud pit tests your resolve. U.S. Navy

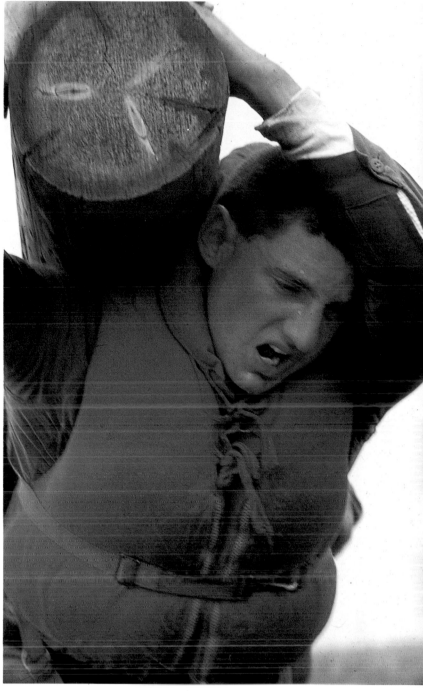

Above: Log PT. U.S. Navy

Left: Here's another station at the "O" course, toward the end. By now your knees are a little wobbly and the muscles in your arms are burning, but you've got to negotiate this wall before you can rest.

Chapter Two

Movement to Contact

Missions: Recon

The very first mission of the very first SEALs, fifty years ago, was reconnaissance. There are many variations on the idea, some very small and covert, others large-scale, long-term studies of terrain, towns, and tactical units. Recons can be done in the water, on the beach, or far inland. The best SEAL recons, though, don't go much past the high water mark; as one SEAL recently said, the best missions for NSW "keep one foot in the water."

There has been a trend away from that attitude and away from the hydrographic survey mission, a change many SEALs find objectionable. But they still train hard to do it (along with the others) and the members of ST1 and 5 performed many beach surveys during Desert Storm. Here's how it works:

It starts with the man they call the CATF—Commander, Amphibious Task Force—the Navy admiral who brings the assault elements to the beach. When the possibility of an assault begins to loom, the CATF directs his staff—the Intelligence officer and the Operations officer, called the N2 and N3—to begin the planning process. The CATF will designate one or many possible beaches for study and consideration.

The N2 and N3 will turn their staffs loose on the problem, at the same time tasking the most available SEAL unit to provide the hydrographic survey information. This will usually be the ARG Platoon, the Amphibious Ready Group. ARG deployments haven't been real popular in the community because there has been a perception that you're going to be out of the action if something cooks off—but that attitude has been changing lately because the ARG platoons have been leading the charge for many recent real world ops.

Left: A miniature submarine called a SEAL Delivery Vehicle (SDV) is readied for launch from a submarine. U.S. Navy

Right: Here's a "Mk 1 Mod 0" Naval Special warrior, complete with aviator's gloves, CAR-15, a Ranger-style assault vest, and a bad case of sea-sickness... no, that's "war paint," artfully applied. SEALs "cammie up" better than anybody. Gary Kieffer/Foto Consortium

No terrorist is safe, even at sea, even on a big ship with its smooth steel sides, from the US Navy SEALs.

This is not a sight to gladden the heart of maritime mischief makers—a SEAL platoon from Group Two (Little Creek, Virginia, is their home port) "takes down" the USNS Joshua Humphries while training for the real thing against Iraq during Operation Desert Shield in the Red Sea. Weapons, uniforms, and equipment carried by the SEALs are completely alien to conventional units. U.S. Navy

"Commo check!" An RTO tests his Motorola MX300. U.S. Navy

The SEAL platoon commander will receive his mission; it will include a description of what the SEALs need to provide, but it will not (or should not) tell the SEALs how to accomplish the mission. The "how" part is something the SEALs get to design.

The platoon will brain-storm the problem, then present a solution back to the Ops and Intel sections; there may be several solutions, or just one. There will be negotiations about resources required. Finally, the plan is pre-sented to the CATF for approval or denial. If denied, the process starts over.

After approval, the mission is scheduled ("laid on" is the operative phrase), and launched at the appointed hour. Insertion will normally be from a CRRC, or patrol boat; the boat will bring the swimmers to 600 to 1,000 meters off the beach, then chuck them overboard. This kind of recon is normally conducted in the water, so the SEALs will execute it as a surface swim, typically at night. The squad swims in, spreads out, and moves in, line abreast. The water depths are charted with a lead line, recorded on a plastic slate. The team, or elements of the group, may move all the way into the beach, recording reefs, rocks, obstacles. Above the high water mark, any fortifications are identified: bunkers, artillery and machine gun positions, plus structures, roads, and any terrain features like sea walls that might prevent the assault force from exiting the beach and driving into the hinterland.

The point man on a patrol communicates silently with hand and arm signals. At the first sign of danger he will freeze; each man following instantly freezes as well. Even so, here he signals HALT.

Beach surveys prior to the kick-off of Operation Desert Storm identified several beaches suitable for landing operations—but all were extremely well defended by Iraqi units, making an actual amphibious assault quite risky. The results of these surveys provided the CATF important and useful information; he elected to merely threaten the assault the enemy expected, pinning the defenders on the shore while the actual attack swept in behind them.

Ship & Oil Platform Takedown

In many ways, SEALs provide a kind of SWAT team resource for the US government. With depressing regularity, nasty people do horrible things to innocent folks on the high seas. Until Dick Marcinko invented and built SEAL Team SIX during the 1980s the United States had virtually nothing to counter terrorists except massive firepower—and massive firepower tends to kill all the hostages along with all the terrorists.

ENEMY IN SIGHT...

But Marcinko's team and the US Army's *Delta Force* counterpart (developed about the same time by Charlie Beckwith) studied Britain's Special Air Service (SAS) tech-

Think about the problem for a moment: how do you put a combat force aboard a ship, for example, out in the ocean? An airplane sitting on an airport taxiway, full of hostages and suicidal gunmen? An oil platform? Into a building full of nervous lunatics with guns and explosives?

All are interesting, important challenges, and all are manageable situations. They were common enough a few years ago. You don't hear much about them anymore because so many terrorists have been killed by the SAS, Delta, SEALs, Spetsnaz, and Israeli counter-terror units that have been so successful in countering every move.

So how do they do it? Well, sorry, we aren't going to tell you—but we will give you some hints and clues. For instance, it is quite possible to sneak aboard a ship, even one underway, quite invisibly. The equipment required is extremely low-tech, available in any large city. No terror-

ONE...

niques for conducting counter-terrorist ops with stealth and surgical precision. Both SIX and Delta quickly learned to conduct counter-terrorist missions quite unlike anything SEALs ever considered before. They learned to assault buildings, sort out good guys from bad guys, and leave only the bad guys with 9mm entrance wounds between the eyebrows. They learned to do this sort of thing in the dark, with the noise and confusion of stun grenades. They learned to make pistols and machine guns virtually silent. They learned how to assault ships, airplanes, oil platforms, buildings of all configurations. Any man on either team became adept at stealthy, speedy movement. They, between them, invented the American version of the art of the "take down."

TAKE COVER...

ist is safe, even at sea, even on a big ship with its smooth steel sides, from the US Navy SEALs. Dressed in black, armed with silenced submachine guns, these men can materialize at any moment, at any point on the deck of the vessel. One at a time, without a noise or a warning, members of the terrorist unit will be identified and "neutralized" one way or another. The standard way is with a bullet to the brain, and it usually works quite well. Terrorists now know that even attempts at surrender at this point are futile—they will die no matter what they do.

The same object lesson has been learned by airplane hijackers. It is quite possible to approach an airliner undetected, then get aboard, sort good people from bad, and kill the bad ones. Sometimes the aircraft is destroyed in the process but many hundreds of hostages have been rescued from gunmen. There are very few surviving hostage-takers—and very, very few hijackings any more.

OFFICER...

Movement to Contact 47

Previous pages left: SEALs have adopted the "drive-on rag" as a kind of unofficial headgear, much to the disgust and dismay of the rest of the Navy. But a cap or floppy hat restrict vision and impede hearing out in the jungle, and the simple triangular bandage, pilfered from a corpsman's supplies, makes a superbly practical headband. It absorbs sweat, cuts the shine from your forehead, breaks up the outline of the body making it a little harder to identify at a distance—and it is part of the old, "bad boy" SEAL image dating back to Viet Nam. Charles Mussi/Foto Consortium

Previous page right: While SEALs normally have fire support on call from artillery and combat aviation, communicating and coordinating with the planes or the gun batteries has become an art and ritual of its own, the "call for fire." During Viet Nam SEALs had their own "organic" helicopter gunship support from Sea Wolf versions of the Huey. Today it comes from the Air Force, Navy, Marines—and who knows, maybe the Russian Air Force will fly cover for the teams in the future.

Point man in the jungle. SEALs travel in the worst, most difficult, and uncomfortable places to discourage detection.

These lessons have been applied to all sorts of tactical situations, including many that fit in between conventional and unconventional warfare. During Operation Ernest Will (a tanker escort mission during the Iran-Iraq war) the Iranians were discovered to be mining the Persian Gulf, an act of war that indiscriminately damaged merchant and naval vessels of several nations, American included.

US Navy P-3 "Orion" surveillance aircraft discovered the culprit, an old landing ship named the *Iran Ajr*, laying the mines on 20 September 1987. The next night two tiny, black, nearly silent AH-6 helicopters (nicknamed the "Sea Bats") from the US Army's counter-ter-

ror/special operations aviation unit called Task Force 160 ("Night Stalkers") found the vessel and watched the crew at work through night vision goggles and a forward-looking-infrared (FLIR) sensor display, radioed their report back to the flagship. At 0023 hours Admiral Harold Bernsen, task force commander, approved a preplanned attack over the KY-57 secure radio link to the "Little Bird" helicopters: *EXECUTE.*

A sniper team with the gigantic .50cal Haskins rifle. SEALs learn the craft of sniping at the Army's Special Warfare Center, located on the back lot at Fort Bragg, North Carolina, along with all the special operators from all the services. Sniper teams learn to virtually disappear, to remain hidden for days, reporting from under the noses of the enemy. If necessary, the sniper can kill a man half a mile away with the first shot from that rifle—up to over a mile, if he's good. And he doesn't get out of the SOTIC (Special Operations Target Interdiction Course) without being less than superb.

From just a few hundred yards the two stealthy helicopters literally "nailed" the Iran Ajr with special Hydra 70 rockets; instead of conventional explosive warheads, some of the 70mm rockets delivered loads of nail-like steel arrows called "fleshettes." Each rocket produces a cloud of these tiny missiles. The effect was immediate and devastating. Most of the Iranian sailors on deck were killed or injured.

Movement to contact. This rifleman models the latest in SEAL fashion, the elegant floppy hat with brim pinned up. The little red device on the muzzle of the rifle is a "blank adapter" used during tactical training exercises. Charles L. Mussl/Foto Consortium

A point man in the jungle.

The helos open up with 7.62mm machine guns, bringing the mine-laying operation to a halt without destroying the vessel or the evidence. The survivors, understanding their predicament, attempt to get the remaining mines off the boat; to prevent them, the AH-6s open fire again, killing some of the crew and starting a small fire on the vessel.

SEALs from the Amphibious Ready Group (ARG) platoon aboard the USS Guadalcanal board the ship at first light, find it abandoned. A search of the waters nearby by Special Boat Unit members aboard Mk III patrol boats

Another kind of movement to contact. This swim pair navigates into the beach with the aid of a compass (or "attack") board. U.S. Navy

Right: Oops, sorry 'bout that. This Iraqi-occupied oil platform was supposed to be taken down by a platoon of SEALs but the pre-raid "softening up" fire support provided by US Army attack helicopters didn't get the word to use only "ball" ammunition. The armor-piercing incendiaries set fire to the platform, preventing the assault. Oh, well, live and learn. U.S. Navy

reveals about two dozen of the surviving crew, some wounded, pathetically trying to evade capture; the SBU crews make the capture—a good example of the kind of teamwork between the SEALs and the Special Boat Unit crews that is the foundation of the NSW tradition. No more mines appeared in the Persian Gulf.

Not all takedowns go so smoothly. A raid on an oil platform, used by Iran to shoot at its neighbors in Gulf waters, kicked off with Army attack helicopters laying down a preliminary suppressive fire. *Unfortunately*, though, the ammunition mix included high explosive/incendiary projectiles and the platform caught fire before the SEALs got to take it down.

If they had their chance, though, the SEALs would have "fast-roped" from helicopters onto the platform, swarming aboard and throughout the structure in a rapid, carefully orchestrated clearing maneuver. Properly done, this kind of assault goes so quickly that defenders are galvanized into inaction, shocked by the sudden appearance of the force, its noise and firepower. Organized resistance is nearly impossible—things happen too quickly for the defender to react.

Disorganized resistance occurs but prisoners are seldom taken when the assault force is opposed.

Despite some glitches and imperfections, American special operations forces have developed weapons, tactics, procedures and acquired the experience to begin to rival the British and Israelis as masters of the art. Thanks to all the Special Operations Forces of many nations, terrorist threats have diminished tremendously since the 1970s and '80s, and the US Navy SEALs have had much to do with the successful campaign.

Receiving the Mission

SEALs are in a service industry; they solve problems for other people—the most senior officers of government. When these people decide that there is a problem, they hand it off to the Navy. Today, SEAL mission taskings trickle down a chain of command that can begin many thousands of miles from Coronado, from

Although SEALs like to keep one foot in the water, their special skills and training sometimes take them well in from the beach. That was especially true after Iraq invaded Kuwait. Then, SEALs were the first combat forces on station and provided crucial "eyes-on" recon services for the National Command Authority, particularly for the Joint Chiefs of Staff and the task force commander. U.S. Navy

Right: The little RIB (Rigid Hull Inflatable boats) got a real workout during Operation Desert Storm. These SEALs are loading an outboard engine prior to a mission. U.S. Navy

the Pentagon or from a theater or task force commander. The problem gets handed to an admiral, handed off to a series of subordinates, until at last it lands on the doorstep of the young officers and enlisted sailors on one of the teams.

Planning for a mission is a group activity. Members of the platoon tasked with the job will participate; so, too, will people from the Group operations staff; the team commander will join in. They brainstorm the problem for hours, or days—or longer. They will typically pull in every kind of information available that will help design the best solution to the problem. If there is lots of time, someone may actually visit the location where a raid or a rescue might occur. Sometimes, as has happened in the past, a prisoner will be snatched out of the objective area, brought back to the compound and interrogated to provide fresh information.

If the mission happens to be one that has been "war-gamed" in the past, a contingency plan might already be on the shelf in the operations section. In fact, a contingency plan for SEAL missions on the island of Grenada was developed several months before Operation Urgent Fury assaulted the defenders of the place in 1982—but the plan was overlooked and not noticed until the mission was concluded.

But normally the plan is prepared in ritual format, then presented to the commander in a dog-and-pony act called a brief-back. The commander is ultimately responsible for the success of the mission, even though he doesn't go along, and he is likely to be quite careful

about the overall intent and the details. He will either accept the plan as designed, accept with modifications he requires, or he may tell the planning group to go back and try it again.

Planning from the Inside Out

"The planning process can take anywhere from a couple of hours to a couple of months," one SEAL says. "It depends on the magnitude of whatever you are trying to do, and the schedule for when you have to complete it. Interestingly, we plan from the center, out—we

begin with the 'actions at the objective,' then work forward and backward from there. That means that we decide where and when we will be on the objective, then we calculate how long it will take us to get there—that tells us when we have to infiltrate—and how long it will take us to get to the extraction point—which tells us when we'll exfiltrate."

There are two basic planning procedures—deliberate and ad hoc. The first is done by the intel section of the community; a target list of possible scenarios is developed and kept ready on the shelf. If North Korea ever decides to invade Argentina, there is probably a contingency plan already on the shelf anticipating the SEALs role in countering it.

"The first thing you feel is excitement—not because you are happy about the mission, but excited because you wonder if you are going to live through the next night. It is an adrenaline rush, but I always felt nervous. That might be because I have been hit a couple of times going in on an operation. Now, I have done open-ocean insertions and riverine insertions—and I much prefer the open ocean as protection from getting ambushed...

SEALs regroup after a ship take-down training session. U.S. Navy

even if I do get seasick! One other thing about open ocean transits—you always get really cold, even in the tropics, because of the wind and spray beating on you."

Once the plan for the mission has been approved by the commander, the squads who will actually be launched on the operation go into isolation. If these squads are working at Coronado or Little Creek that means no more phone calls, no chance to go home to kiss the wife and kids good-bye, no chance to compromise the op before it even gets started.

All the assets are laid on: weapons, dive gear, boats, aircraft, ammunition, demo material, maps—the works.

The players begin rehearsing the operation, if time permits.

In the contemporary world, with no-notice, short-fuse conflicts being the norm, planning for missions is quite different than during Viet Nam, World War II, or even during Desert Storm, when platoons developed and executed their own operations.

SPECWARCOM gets a tasking, then hands that off to a suitable SEAL team. That team then develops a proposed course of action—or several options—for presentation to the commander.

There is something of a tradition in NSW of having teams and team leaders tasked with missions that just won't work. Part of the history of the SEALs is a long list of missions that have been ill-conceived, badly executed, and fatal to a high proportion of the people participating. The attack on the airfield at Patilla in Panama was one of these; the night parachute drop just before Urgent Fury kicked off was another. These disasters are

often imposed on the teams by conventional force commanders who don't always understand the limits of what a team can do. But there is another tradition within the SEAL community, one where junior officers stand up and say, in effect, that a particular plan is a "no-go." As one old SEAL says: "There is a difference between being given a mission and being told how to accomplish it. Once, in Viet Nam, I was given a mission that was obviously extremely dangerous and that didn't seem to be very well thought out. When I asked for more information about the operation, the captain told me, 'all I can

tell you is that it will give you a shot at a Medal of Honor.'

"I told him, 'the only Medal of Honor recipients I know of are dead—so until I get more information about this thing, don't count me in on it.' Eventually, somebody else got the mission, and he died trying to accomplish it. Like so many times in our history, there were too many people trying to get involved, too many folks trying to get in on the glory."

SEALs patrolled well inland along the Iraq/Saudi border during the first weeks after the invasion, until heavy Marine and Army ground force units could be deployed. Living and operating conditions were nothing short of appalling, with temperatures in the 120s and humidity to match. U.S. Navy

Chapter Three

What the Well-Dressed SEAL Wears to the Party

When the real world calls the SEAL community with a mission, dive equipment lockers, weapons storage rooms, ammunition and explosive storage bunkers, and team equipment rooms are unlocked and looted of their contents. SEALs have far more latitude and personal discretion in the selection of weapons, load-bearing equipment, and mission-specialized gear than conventional forces. Conventional Army and Navy units issue only the M9 Beretta 9mm pistol, for example, while SEALs may carry Sig-Sauers, Hechler & Koch P-9s or P-7s, or any of several other sidearms never seen outside of the spec op community. Assault vests, invented by the Israelis and popular with special operators everywhere, adorn SEALs, Army Rangers, and "Green Berets" in place of conventional LBE (Load-Bearing Equipment) harness issued by the government. SEALs normally buy their own vests, often custom built to order by retired SEALs.

A SEAL's uniform is also likely to be as unconventional as the mission; aviator's flight suits are popular attire, on the ground and in the water, and are even worn over wet suits on some combat swim operations. The standard Battle Dress Uniform (called "BDU") in both the "woodland" green and brown pattern, and the desert pattern are also popular—then it can be difficult to sort the SEALs out from the rest of the troops. There are also outfits for high-altitude parachute jumps, wet and dry suits for dive operations—and civilian clothes for special occasions.

Basic Load

When you suit up to go off to play hide-and-seek in the weeds with the opposing team, you literally bet your life

Left: The DPV carries a crew of three, a driver, commander, and a gunner. It carries nearly as much firepower as the new 170ft patrol boats: a .50 caliber machine gun, 40mm grenade launcher, 7.62mm M-60 machine-gun, and anti-air or anti-armor missiles.

Right: Although it doesn't look nearly so cool, the tactically correct way to carry belts of ammunition for your M-60 are in these pouches on the gunner's H harness, not in glittering belts across the chest.

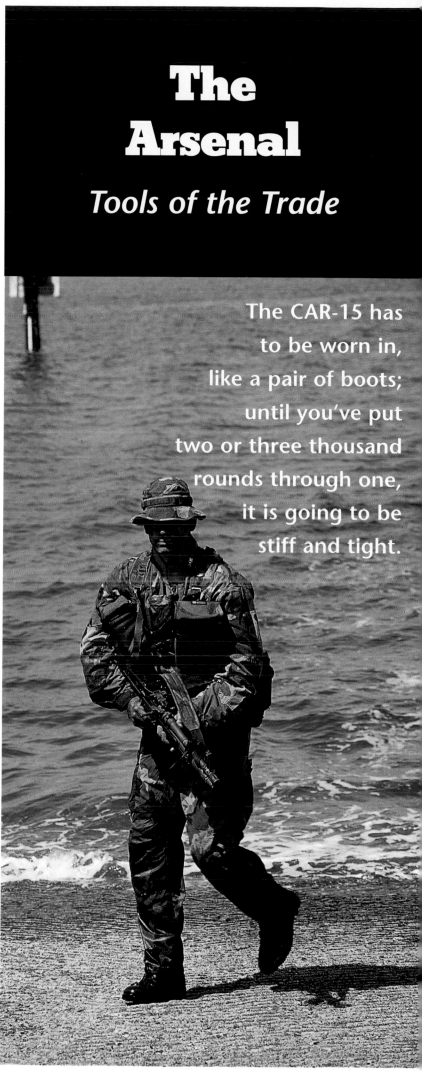

The Arsenal

Tools of the Trade

The CAR-15 has to be worn in, like a pair of boots; until you've put two or three thousand rounds through one, it is going to be stiff and tight.

on every single thing you wear or carry. SEALs have developed some pretty standard collections of gear for all sorts of social occasions—and if you are new at this, it pays to listen closely to the counsel of your old senior chief petty officers and do exactly what they advise. Here is a summary of what they suggest:

First, think of your gear in three groups. The first, and most essential will be your clothing and your weapon. Use the pockets to store absolute survival essentials. This primary group is called *First Line* equipment.

First Line Equipment

First Line gear includes your boots, socks, uniform, hat, scarf and gloves—the things you wear during the entire operation. Your personal weapon and one magazine of ammunition are also included in this group. So, too, are the most critical items required for survival: map, watch, money (local and American), a compass, a condom (*pri-*

Fresh from a boat ride, this M-14 equipped rifleman still wears his personal flotation device (PFD). Hard experience has shown that even SEALs can drown when loaded heavily enough, and even when equipped with this little life saver; when the loads get really heavy, everybody wears two PFDs.

marily for waterproofing, not for visits to the local ladies—except in emergencies), a recognition panel for signaling aircraft, a signal mirror, pocket knife, and 25ft of "dummy cord" (as parachute suspension line is called). Somewhere in your pockets, too, you will need an emergency medical kit with codeine, morphine, a battle dressing (for sucking chest wounds), and an ace bandage. An MRE (Meal, Ready to Eat) or a couple of commercial "Power Bars" will get you by for a day or two of escape and evasion. A little flashlight, wire saw, and whistle, matches, and 12ft of tubular nylon to tie a "Swiss seat" are also recommended parts of the First Line package of fashion accessories. With this much gear—even if everything else is lost—your training, your knowledge of the local terrain and culture, you ought to be able to avoid capture for several days or more while you follow your E&E (escape and evasion) plan.

Second Line Equipment

Your Second Line gear goes into your combat vest or load-bearing equipment. This equipment allows you to work and fight efficiently: magazines and ammunition, grenades, and handcuffs for dealing with enemy personnel go into the vest or on your LBE. Insect repellent, a day's worth of rations, a strobe light with filter, two-quart canteen and water purification tablets, another battle dressing, a knife, a snap link, and a medical kit are all tucked into pouches on this LBE.

Third Line Equipment

Your rucksack contains Third Line gear: radios and batteries, a section of cammo net six feet square, water bladders or bottles, demolition material, Claymore mine, poncho and liner, ground sheet, and spare uniform. This group of gear will vary with the responsibilities and the preferences of the individual. A corpsman will bring along enough medical supplies in his ruck to treat major trauma, including bags of Ringers' lactate solution and the catheter kits for IVs, airways, Penrose drains, more battle dressings, and a lot more. Some members of the patrol will likely include night vision goggles (NVG), bolt cutters, an entrenching tool, PRC-90 rescue radios, a water filter, binoculars, or machete.

If the rucksack gets ditched (as it might, for example, during a pursuit of the team by an enemy force), each member can still fight effectively and drive on with just Line One and Two gear. Even if Line Two gear has to be abandoned, each SEAL can still escape and evade with just Line One equipment. It is a system that makes sense, and it works—just ask the old senior chiefs.

Personal Weapons

Special operators are well-known for using a wide variety of non-standard issue weapons, and SEALs are notori-

Commander Gary Stubblefield, former commander of SEAL Team 3, prepares to enter the frigid Pacific Ocean. The chrome strip on his mask is taped to kill the shine, he wears a medium-weight wet suit under his utilities, and is equipped with a Draeger re-breather. The number "113" is Cdr. Stubblefield's BUD/S student number; it has been about twenty-five years since he survived the experience, but the number will follow him forever.

ous for taking the practice to extremes. AK-47s were quite popular with team members in Viet Nam, as was the Soviet-designed RPD. This latter weapon is a really superb light machine gun—balanced, reliable, effective.

Automatic weapons have characteristic sounds and tracer colors that are easily recognized in combat. When you use an adversary's tools against him, he can often be

The lieutenant leads a SEAL platoon. Here he's going through his "Line 2" gear from his H harness: a 500ml bag of Ringer's Lactate for IVs, a M-18 red smoke grenade for signaling, poncho liner, flare, and first aid kit are all visible. He also carries five 30-round mags for the CAR-15, light sticks, a tiny radio to back up the RTO, and a small survival kit. Robert Genat/Zone Five Photo

confused into thinking that he is in a "friendly fire" engagement with his own units. If he hesitates as a result you can take the initiative against him. This is a technique that works—just ask the senior chiefs.

CAR-15

The CAR-15 is a compact version of the standard M16 rifle. Both have been around longer than just about anybody left on active duty—more than thirty years for the M16. The CAR-15 uses a shorter barrel and a collapsible stock but otherwise shares the basics of the M16. That includes, of course, the .223 caliber (cal) cartridge. That little bullet comes out of the muz-

zle at extremely high velocity. It is accurate, extremely effective when it hits, and produces a quite mild recoil. The light, compact nature of the ammunition permit a SEAL to carry far more rounds for the same weight penalty as an M60 gunner.

You can take it into the water but you'd better sand-proof it before taking it through the surf on a combat swim. The normal procedure for this is to cap the muzzle with either a cover or a condom, then apply silicon sealant around the magazine and the bolt cover. Once on the beach each member of the

Right: The PRC-112 is a little UHF survival/rescue radio originally designed for air crew. Its range is strictly line-of-sight, its frequency limited to 121.5 MHz, but that's all you need to call in the helicopters to get you out of the jungle—if the helicopters are overhead. It only weighs a pound and a half. A similar radio was the only thing that saved one team along the Ho Chi Minh trail when their primary PRC-77 absorbed some VC bullets. But it transmits a beacon every US military aircraft monitors on "guard" channel so if a C-130 comes floating by way overhead, you can get his attention.

security element will, in turn, drain and check his weapon for proper function before proceeding with the mission; a functional weapon is one of those mission-essential items.

"The CAR-15 is one of the finest military weapons ever made," says one combat veteran SEAL. "It is a very high-precision weapon (unlike the AK-47) and if it isn't kept clean, though, it can give you problems. So it has to be treated properly, sealed against sand and mud before an insertion. Another thing about the weapon—it has to be worn in, like a pair of boots; until you've put two or three thousand rounds through one, it is going to be stiff and tight. In Viet Nam we even loosened up the chamber a little bit. The other important thing is, you can learn to keep them meticulously clean—keep the dust cover closed and the muzzle sealed with a condom, for example.

"The .223 round is a high-velocity, low-mass projectile; it had a bad reputation for a while when people thought

This little Motorola MX300 radio is a big hit with the teams. It is set up here with throat mike and ear piece, both excellent for quick, convenient, quiet communications during ship or platform take-downs, patrols, recons, or assaults.

Believe it or not, this little box is a war-winner. It is Magellan's version of the Global Positioning System (GPS) receiver, a technological innovation that has transformed the capabilities of SEALs and any other force that possesses GPS. Turn the receiver on, then push POS; within a couple of minutes the GPS will display your current position on the surface of the earth to within about 50 feet—a tremendous increase in precision over earlier methods. SEALs use it to identify targets and fixed objects as well as to navigate on water and land.

The standard old UDT black rubber mask has gradually been displaced by commercial masks for sport diving. That was fine until recently because the cost was low and the quality high; the masks on the market are still well designed and well made—but they are only available in screaming bright neon colors of red, purple, and yellow, none of which are particularly good for clandestine operations.

that any kind of leaf or twig would deflect it, and that such a small bullet wouldn't produce an incapacitating wound. But when you hit something with that little bullet at that high velocity, the hydrostatic shock can be extremely effective. It is highly accurate, very reliable. The problem with the weapon, when there is one, is likely to be with the person carrying it."

The amount of ammunition carried on a mission will vary with the nature of the op; five to seven 30-round magazines are typical, though, providing between 150 to 210 rounds per rifleman.

M-203

There are some targets that you just can't hit with a rifle, no matter how good a shot you are. When the bad guys are snuggled in on the back side of a hill, a berm or a rice paddy dike—or when they are buckled into a bunker with a machine gun—you can plink at them all day with your trusty CAR-15 and never score a point.

Now, with conventional forces, this is the time when you make the "call for fire," a request for artillery or air fire support. SEALs, though, often don't have that option—the mission is a strictly "do it yourself" operation. And the M-203 is a really handy little indirect fire support weapon.

The "203" isn't much more than a simple aluminum tube and breech mechanism. It is a single shot, 40mm weapon. It throws a projectile about twice the size of a golf ball (and considerably smaller than a baseball) out several hundred meters with excellent accuracy. Its velocity is fairly slow, the trajectory much more of an arc than a straight line, and you can watch it fly out toward its target. Now you can start beating up on those pesky guys on the back side of the berm; you can pump a few HE (high explosive) rounds through a bunker aperture where a machine gun crew is feeling safe and sound; you can lob a CS (tear gas) round into a room where a sniper is barricaded—and you will defeat them all with the M-203.

The grenadier is one of the most tactically valuable men on the squad. Besides the HE rounds, he carries illumination rounds to light up the night, star shells and smoke rounds for signaling, and a dual purpose HE-incendiary round for use against light-skinned vehicles and other suitable targets.

"The 203 is a wonderful weapon for folks out in the woods who need a little extra firepower and don't have anybody to call on for immediate fire support."

M-60 E3

SEALs use a lightweight, cut-down version of the same M-60 light machine gun used by Marines and soldiers, designated the M-60 E3. Yet, while conventional units consider the gun a crew-served weapon, requiring two beefy men for its care and feeding, SEALs manage the gun all alone. Back in the ancient days in southeast Asia, when the weapon was still fairly new, some since-forgotten SEAL armorer took a hacksaw to the machine gun and cut several pounds away. Now, you can't get away with that in the 82d Airborne Division, but the special ops community was a different story, then and now. Well, the modification was successful enough that it is no longer something the team armorers have to do; now,

The Sig Sauer 9mm pistol is a great favorite of SEALs for its reliable functioning. This one is carried in a strapped-down "drop" holster that appears to be home-brewed by the guys who run the parachute loft. Two 15-round mags are carried horizontally above the holster flap. If you ever get into a fight that takes more than forty-five rounds for your pistol, you are in a very bad place indeed.

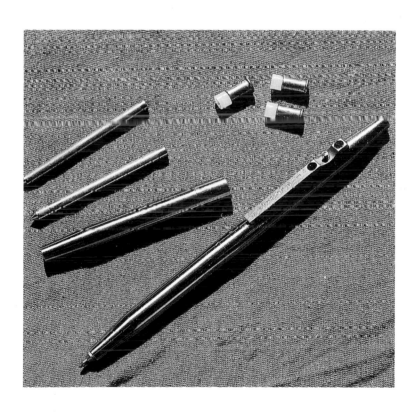

"Okay, okay, I will sign your darn confession—just let me use my own pen." Now here's a weapon you won't see every day—or any day if the Public Affairs Officer has any thing to say about it. SEALs don't use anything like this while working for the regular Navy or while assigned to SPECWARCOM, but some SEALs go off to "black" programs where they go nameless places to do secret things. That's not something any SEAL will discuss, but once in a while somebody will pull out one of these things with a wink and a nudge. It uses .22 caliber blanks to propel either a regular ball point cartridge, or an alloy dart (top).

the design is fully approved and available off the shelf from a manufacturer.

Even with the liposuction, it is still a heavy gun—18.5lb empty, about 5lb lighter than the standard version. A belt of 100 linked rounds, ready to fire, adds another 7lb to the gunner's burden, and he will probably carry at least two such belts. Although the weapon fires at a rate of about 550 rounds per minute, you can't keep that up for long without burning out the barrel and "cooking off" rounds; the M-60's sustained rate of fire is actually only 100 rounds per minute. The machine gunner tends to be the biggest, beefiest guy on the squad, for good reason.

There's no good reason, though, for something you see quite often, the sight of a SEAL all cammied up but with two shiny belts of 7.62 NATO rounds for the M-60 draped like bandoleers across his chest. Not only does all this bright brass attract the eye of everybody within a mile, it tends to kink the belt, bend the links, and get the rounds dirty, resulting in failure-to-feed problems with the gun. It is a bit like wearing a sign that says "shoot me." But, it really does look cool in photographs.

"I see guys with these bandoleers of ammo across their chest so often now that it is commonplace. It drives me ballistic," said one SEAL. "I shame them into doing it correctly, but I think this is a symptom of a training mentality. We haven't had to operate in a real world environment for long periods for a long time and those lessons have been forgotten."

SEAL machine gunners normally rig the ammunition belts in packs that ride on the upper portion of the LBE or combat vest, sometimes with feed trays to guide the belt and protect it from twists and kinks. Another alternative is to rig the ammo on the back, feeding the belt over the shoulder. When firing from the prone position the belt will normally be draped across the left forearm of the gunner.

Machine guns like the M-60 are area weapons, delivering a large volume of fire to a target that might be a whole squad, a crew-served weapon, or an enemy unit that has just walked into the kill zone of an ambush. While the rounds will kill out to about two miles, any hits out that far are strictly luck; 1,000 meters is the practical limit for targets you can beat up effectively.

H&K MP-5

While Americans have always had a traditional fondness for their long-range precision marksmanship, the trend in real-world operations has been toward close-quarters combat. This kind of combat often occurs in crowded urban environments, inside airplanes, or in places where many innocents may be endangered. Consequently, SWAT teams, civil and military both, have traded their big rifles for little submachine guns. And today just about everybody agrees that the German firm of Heckler & Koch makes the very best.

"The MP-5 is great for close-in situations, especially where you have to swim ashore—but its maximum effective range, in my experience, is only 25 yards," one SEAL said. "Most of us like them because they are very reliable. We like them, too, because you can make them *almost* silent.

"The 9mm round is notorious for its lack of stopping power, but I maintain that *any* round will do the job. After all, the little .22 long rifle cartridges kill many people every year. The important thing is *shot placement*. The only way to make the 9mm more effective is to use bullets like police officers do, the Black Talon and HydraShok projectiles that expand on impact. But the Geneva Convention prohibits us from using those, so we are stuck with standard 'hard ball' fully jacketed rounds. It's pitiful."

Shotgun

"The shotgun is the single most effective close-in weapon we have today," a SEAL reported. "Even so, very few team members will ever use it—and I don't know why. Maybe it is because you can only get five rounds in it. We have tried all sorts of things to boost capacity, including a

drum magazine. But nothing will stop a person better than a shotgun!"

The weapon is not only effective against people, it works against all sorts of targets that resist other projectiles—like vehicle engines, for example. SEALs carry a few "slug" rounds, heavy lead projectiles encased in a plastic

Here's the SEALs own little dune buggy, a modified off-road racer quite able to blow the doors off the competition. SEALs used the DPV (Desert Patrol Vehicle) to cruise deep into Iraqi held territory, cruise the border, and to provide pilot rescue services if required.

The commo gear really got a work-out during Desert Storm, with units deployed across a huge landscape and lots of competition for channels on the satcoms. U.S. Navy

sabot, for such targets. One of these will punch a hole through the side of a car or truck—and keep on going right into the engine block, bringing a halt to the proceedings. The slug round has another handy application, opening doors; when you come knocking with one of these, the door will come open no matter how unfriendly the folks inside.

Then there's the traditional buckshot rounds, a load of small lead balls in "double-ought" or "four-ought" (00 or 0000 size). The latter round puts out twenty-four .22-caliber lead pellets that has a devastating effect on whatever is coming at you. If you are the guy on point in the jungle,

or going into a room-clearing situation, there is nothing better; an oddly under-used weapon.

M-14 Rifle

The M-14 is an accurate, interesting weapon that is even older than the M-16. Designed to replace the World War II M-1 Garand, the M-14 fires a slightly smaller .30-caliber cartridge, the 7.62 NATO round. It was issued to US Army units for just a few years before being replaced by the M-16 and its radical, high-velocity little projectile.

"The M-14 is a highly touted team weapon, beloved for its reliability and its long-range penetrating power," says a SEAL. "My point, though, is—how often do you see people shoot at more than fifty meters? It just doesn't happen often, and then you need the sniper specialists with

The AN/PSN-9 is a man-pack GPS system with 18m precision, even better than the little hand-held versions. It is a lot heavier, though, and for that reason has somewhat limited use. It is, however, just one of the many systems SEALs have in the gear lockers for any contingency.

the .50cal. It's heavy, bulky, and the rounds are heavy, too; I'll take the M-16 any day."

But SEALs and a few other specialized units retain some of the M-14s as a kind of intermediate sniper weapon. Its practical effective range (with a good shooter on a good day under ideal wind, light, and terrain conditions) is up to about 500 meters. That doesn't mean that the weapon can't hit targets accurately out to 1,000 meters, because it certainly can; but combat shooting is a completely different kind of qualification course on a different kind of range than anybody experiences on a training range.

Radios

"Our radios are improving at an almost exponential rate, in terms of reliability and capability," according to one SEAL. "And, with increased range and reliability, the size hasn't increased. Radios today are better than ever, more interoperable—and, even so, we *still* have communications problems! So we have a habit of having a backup plan, and that means that today we have more radios in a squad

SEALs train to make night parachute jumps with long delays and low altitude openings. This little gadget makes sure the parachute opens before you plow into the ground.

M-16 (not the CAR-15) and M203 40mm grenade launcher. The veil has two functions: it prevents light from reflecting from the skin, and it makes the gunner unrecognizable. SEALs are notorious for a desire to stay out of the press. Gary L. Kieffer/ Foto Consortium

than ever before. I think that's a waste of time; you need one, or maybe two radios, max, and enough batteries. But sometimes we have a tendency to think if one of something is good, then more is better. That's not the usually the case.

"When I deploy as a platoon commander, I carry my squad radios with me, either one or two, depending on how many squads I am controlling. During ship take-downs, for instance, where we used four squads on the operation, I carried two—one to use with two of the squads, another for the other pair. That allows me to separate the information going to the port and starboard sides, for instance, keeping the information overload problem for the maneuver elements down. But, when it came time to call back to the higher command I relied on my RTO and the radio he carried. He might make the call, but he is required to repeat exactly what I tell him, not an interpretation. If I say, 'tell them the helicopter is coming in from the wrong direction,' he has to say, '*be advised that the helicopter is coming in from the wrong direction*,' and nothing else.

"Most of the radios we use today are not as 'tactical' as they were in the old days. For example, now when we want to talk to our higher headquarters, we have to stop and set up an OP, put everybody into a defensive perimeter, and set up the antennas before we can call back to the

shop. In the old days, before these new, high-speed radios, we could talk on the march through a radio relay station we'd set up—either on a boat or an airplane—somewhere nearby. The radios now make the relay unnecessary, and can talk around the world, but take extra effort and pre-

M-60 gunner laying down a base of fire. Charles Mussi/Foto Consortium

Here is what the well-dressed HALO jumper wears to the operation: two special parachutes, an oxygen supply and mask, rucksack, and folding stock AK-74 tucked under the left arm. Gary Kieffer/Foto Consortium

cautions that slow you down. We can communicate very well now, but at the sacrifice of a little mobility."

GPS

An age-old problem in warfare is knowing where you are at any given moment, a problem that has recently been pretty well solved with the development of the Global Positioning System (GPS). The foundation for this technol-

ogy is a network of twenty-one satellites orbiting the earth; signals from three of these satellites can be processed with compact, hand-held devices to yield position fixes within about 100 meters; when the receiver is programmed to look for four satellites, accuracy increases to just 35 meters—and altitude information is provided as well.

The receivers provide even more than accurate position data, they help the user navigate from one point to another with great precision. GPS systems make fire support much more accurate. The devices not only tell you which way to move between waypoints but how fast you are going at any given moment. If you happen to be a mile or so offshore, moving toward a hostile shore on a cold, foggy night, with a wind blowing and a strong current running, you previously would have to navigate by dead reckoning—a calculated, educated guess. The current and wind will constantly push you off your intended track line, and you will just have to estimate the drift. GPS has changed that; now you can tell exactly where you are, and what course to steer, to reach the map coordinates for your insertion point. The little device tells you the range, bearing, and speed you are making while en route. It has changed the way many people do many military things.

"GPS is the single greatest technological innovation in modern warfare—better than any weapon, better than any radio, better than any boat that has come along," one SEAL said. "It is simply the greatest thing that has ever happened to us. Now, for the first time, we know exactly where we are at any given moment, without any landmarks. We can come back to a spot and find it exactly—within 35 meters. If I recon a beach and I want to come back with my troops, I can now come back to that spot in the dark and find it precisely. If I put a beacon on somebody's doorstep or bunker roof and want somebody to come over and bomb it, I can tell them within 35 meters where to look for that beacon."

GPS receivers are available from several manufacturers, and some designs are modified for SEAL applications. Combat swimmers, for example, take along a water-proofed system for some insertion missions.

While providing tremendous improvements in navigation, GPS still has some limitations. Current models require you to come to the surface for a position fix, and to stay there for at least a minute or so while the GPS receiver looks for its satellites, down-loads and processes data, and then displays the updated position. So while current models require the antenna to be out of the water during processing, NSW RDT&E staff (part of the SPECWARCOM headquarters operation at Coronado) is working on ways to use GPS from below the surface.

Desert Patrol Vehicle (DPV)

The DPV is in some ways a very odd piece of gear to find in the US Navy SEALs bag of tricks. It is a dune buggy with a bad attitude, an 80mph off-road rocket very much like the Volkswagen-powered playthings fabricated by hobbyists who want to play in the sand. The machine is, itself, quite conventional (compared to other dune buggies); the odd part is that it is used by the SEALs.

You can't bring it ashore on a swim; it won't fit in a rubber duck; it might fit in a sub's dry deck shelter. It really doesn't have much to do with the water or with the SEALs traditional maritime missions, looking instead more like something the Marines or Army would want to use. It is, in fact, a symptom of what some old SEALs call the "greening" of the SEAL community, a shift in focus away from the water and the mud, inland to missions that used to be the province of the Army, particularly the SEALs' Army counterparts, the "Green Berets."

But SEALs have been getting tasked with these missions, and they've done them very well in Desert Storm: pilot rescue, long-range recon, patrolling "danger-close" to enemy forces. The DPV is a dream machine for these jobs, even if they are far from the beach. At least it lets you get back to the beach in a hurry!

Originally called the Fast Attack Vehicle, the DPV has been around for about ten years. The prototypes were in fact tested by the Army's "Toys R Us" division in the 1980s. Three SEALs crew the DPV, a commander, a driver and a gunner. It's a two-wheel drive machine with generous ground clearance (16in), a huge skid pan, and outboard racks for carrying gear, supplies, or rescued air crew.

Although no two are likely to be tricked out exactly the same way, the basic weapons suite include a M2 .50cal heavy machine gun, two M-60 light machine guns, and one Mk 19 grenade launcher. A couple of AT-4 anti-armor rocket launchers are normally found stowed on the roll bar; the AT-4 is a good bunker-busting weapon and will reliably kill light armored scout cars, personnel carriers, and the occasional tank—if you make a lucky hit. Stinger anti-air missiles, M203s, and many other weapons often go along for the ride. A Magellan GPS 1000 will likely be installed on the dash, providing precise navigation information to the driver: exact position (to within about 100ft), speed, bearing to target, distance to target, and range to target.

The DPV has 21 gallons (gal) of fuel aboard in internal tanks, enough for 210 miles of normal driving. That capacity can be boosted to 120gal with the addition of a fuel bladder, increasing the range to about 1,000 miles. Three of the vehicles will fit in a C-130 aircraft; they can be dropped by parachute or airlanded, as needed. The vehicle is built by Chenowyth Racing, of El Cajon, California. Power comes from a 200hp VW engine that rockets the DPR from zero to 30mph in just four seconds.

The DPVs currently are only operated by SEAL Team THREE—which is appropriate since Team THREE has plenty of genuine desert to patrol out at Niland, California, where a training compound is available for such joy rides.

DPVs typically operate in little desert rat packs of two or more; since their operational area is normally way out in front of all the friendly forces, and sometimes right in the bad guy's back yard, it is a good idea to have a little mutual support, just in case. One important mission for which the vehicle was designed is Combat Search and Rescue (CSAR)—pilot rescue

Standard attire for close-quarter combat and building clearance missions: MP-5 submachine gun, MX300 with throat mike and ear piece, aviator's flight suit, and goggles. Gary Kieffer/Foto Consortium

from hostile territory, where the ability to get in and back out again in a hurry is a top priority. It is a remarkably agile, speedy, and capable vehicle, able to climb up and down quite extreme terrain features. Now, if they could just make it swim!

Swim Gear
Draeger Mk V

SEALs don't normally use SCUBA gear—except when they are on vacation. SCUBA gear, of the type used by sport divers, is called "open circuit" apparatus; it emits bubbles and noise, both of which can tip off an alert

A SEAL squad can drop in on folks any time, any place. These use steerable MC-1 canopies that permit the jumper to "fly" toward the intended drop zone. Ordinarily, a parachute insertion would only be conducted at night, but training jumps are common, particularly when somebody wants to make photographs. Gary Kieffer/Foto Consortium

enemy to the presence of a clandestine approach by combat swimmers. Instead, a closed-circuit rig has been used since the early Italian combat swims of 1941.

The current rig (in use since 1975) is Austrian in design, although it replaces a very similar system of American manu-

A SEAL preparing for a dive first dons the equipment, opens the O^2 bottle, and carefully purges the system of air. The oxygen flows from the bottle, through a regulator, to the mouthpiece; when the diver exhales, some oxygen and carbon dioxide is exhaled. This mixture is recycled through the canister of baralyme where the CO^2 is absorbed and purified oxygen passed back to the mouthpiece. Only the oxygen actually consumed by the diver needs to be replaced from the tank—a rather small amount—and none of it is wasted.

The tiny cylinder holds about 13 cubic feet of oxygen at 2000 pounds per square inch (psi). While a SCUBA diver would consume this much air in just a few minutes below, a SEAL wearing a Draeger can stay down for hours. Just how long depends a lot on what that SEAL is up to—how deep he goes, how hard he works, how full of adrenaline he happens to be. If he is just trying to avoid one of the senior chiefs who is looking for guys for a detail, he can hide under a dock for half a day. But if he is on a real-world operation, with tracers flying overhead and blood in the water, and the need to dive down to 30ft or so, that tank of O^2 will empty pretty fast.

Ashore, the Draeger is a pretty heavy piece of gear: about 35lb, complete, but in the water it becomes about neutral. It is bulky, and that bulk has to be pushed through the water, so it takes some work to use on a long insertion.

"Although this system has been around for over twenty years, it has been so reliable and so safe that it is still the standard today," a SEAL said. "You can actually get up to four hours use with them, under ideal situations. But the biggest lessons we have learned and not learned well enough yet—is that when you put people under stress, in a real-world situation, gas consumption *doubles* over what you see in tests and hard training. It is something we have to keep rediscovering and working into our planning for real-world events."

One of those real-world events occurred during Operation Just Cause, the invasion of Panama, when Norm Carley's swimmers used the Draegers to swim under much of Balboa harbor on a classic ship attack mission during the opening ceremonies of the little war. Four swimmers placed Mk 138 demo charges on the propeller shaft of Noriega's presidential yacht, the Presidente Porras. Despite some glitches with the operation, the swimmers executed their role perfectly, and when the charges detonated, the engine of the vessel was nearly launched into orbit. But it was an exciting and memorable evening for the four SEALs, requiring a fair amount of escape and evasion; the Draegers worked perfectly—but there wasn't much left in the gas bottles when they were finally hauled back in the rubber ducks.

Mask

The original UDT swimmers of World War II didn't bother with masks at all; it was believed—and with reason—that the reflection from the face plate might attract the attention of an undesirable element. But masks have been standard issue ever since the 1950s and any possi-

facture called the Emerson. The basic concept has been around for fifty years, in one form or another, and it still works better than anything else for the kind of work SEALs have to do. These devices all use a supply of oxygen, a system of bags and hoses, and a canister of a material called baralyme.

A member of SEAL Team 5 models the latest in day wear for frogmen ashore. Note the subtle combinations of green, green, black, brown, and green—set off perfectly with the light green mottled assault vest from SOMAV, nicely accessorized with the classic black CAR-15 from the house of Colt. Gary Kieffer/Foto Consortium

ble drawbacks from possible reflections have been countered by better underwater visibility.

Until fairly recently, SEALs were issued the same old "Mk 1 Mod 0" black rubber design used during the time

of the Korean war. For years it was issued in one size—and fit one guy out of the sixteen on the squad. Then, in the 1970s, some SEALs who were commercial SCUBA instructors on the side started "infiltrating" equipment designed for the sport diver market. Masks became available in ten or so sizes and the fit improved for many on the teams. Now, though, a new problem has surfaced—the design of the commercial masks is terrific, but the only colors available are fashionable "day-glow" reds, oranges, yellows and greens that are intended to attract attention. Basic black is disappearing as an option. Some SEALs are using the bright masks, but taping or painting over the florescent colors. "We'll probably have to contract with some manufacturer to make some in black or dark green," one officer comments, "and then we'll probably have to pay $100 apiece for them."

Flippers

The same problem is occurring with flippers, long purchased as off-the-shelf items from sport dive manufacturers. RDT&E staff has run extensive tests over the years on different models, trying to determine which designs are superior, but the jury is still out. Some prefer one-piece designs with a solid heel strap, others like the adjustable models. The latter have the virtue of being repairable when the strap breaks (which they do, invariably at the worst possible moment) and they can be adjusted to be used with dive booties or combat boots. Experienced operators especially like the latter—and carry spare straps on every dive.

While the fins provide extra speed and power in the water, they are a real pain anywhere else. Among the most awkward problems they create is when you're preparing to launch yourself and a rubber duck out of a C-130 for a water parachute jump. The duck goes out first, and you should follow it closely but that is very difficult with the fins on—and the fins are worn out of the aircraft every time. One way to cope with that is to use "hundred-mile-an-hour" adhesive tape to pull the ends of the fins up and attach them to the leg with a length of the tape; that lets you walk somewhat normally while you exit the bird.

"A long time ago, we used to attach the fins to our web gear belt," a SEAL said. "We would run out of the aircraft, and when the parachute opened, we were supposed to put the fins on; well, there were a lot of fins lost that way! Then we started wearing them, and trying to run out—but a lot of guys tripped. You really need to be right

Above: The M-18 smoke grenade—old reliable, sometimes the only thing that can get the choppers in to haul your ass out of Dodge. Everybody on an op usually carries one.

behind that boat, though, or you will never find it in the water, so that's when we started taping up the ends, and it seems to work really well."

Wet and Dry Suits

The earliest wet suits were really wet—the World War II beach surveys in the Pacific and the Normandy beach clearance missions were done in plain swim trunks and cotton overalls. Neither provided much protection against cold or abrasion, but there wasn't much choice at the time.

There is a choice now, between neoprene wet suits and coated nylon dry suits, each with virtues and vices. Wet suits are standard; they provide good thermal protection under a wide range of conditions; they're durable and last for many years; they are fairly inexpensive and easily repaired. Dry suits provide even more thermal protection, but they are rather delicate and bulky. The zippers are subject to failure and the suits can tear or abrade, and once they start to leak they are useless.

Wet suits, consequently, are used most often. The first ones were off-the-rack, standard size suits that didn't really fit all that well. Later, custom suits for each SEAL were purchased by the teams that fit each man perfectly. BDUs are typically worn over the wet suits for swimmers conducting over-the-beach ops; you can't go very far over the beach in the outfit without roasting, but for a security team (for example) who will be in and out of the water it is a reasonable rig.

"I prefer a wet suit under nearly all situations; they are just so much more flexible," a SEAL said. "The exception to that would have to be when I am on an SDV—the dry suit is a lot warmer. The problem with wet suits is, though, in real-world ops, is that you sometimes have

It isn't too often a combat swimmer gets to come back aboard a sub in daylight, on the surface—well, maybe today is the easy day. Hypothermia, the lowering of the body's temperature, is one of the most dangerous elements of SEAL operations. Standard, commercial wet suits (custom fit, however) have worked well for SEALs and some manage to keep them serviceable for a whole career. U.S. Navy

to wear your uniform under your suit (for an insertion), and you just can't do that with a wet suit. When we started custom-fitting suits to each man, our ability to tolerate really cold water improved tremendously. I have a suit that was issued in 1970; it still fits and still is serviceable. They are really good suits!"

gauge, and watch attached to the board. It's like the instrument panel on a boat at night—the compass tells you direction and the watch tells you how far you've gone; the depth gauge is a safety device that also helps predict oxygen consumption.

All combat swims are done by pairs of divers; one will be the navigator and will use the attack board and steer the "boat" while the other swims alongside, typically with one hand on the navigator's shoulder.

"We have gone through many compass designs over the years, looking for the perfect one," according to one SEAL. "It is the single most important thing on the attack board; it needs to be centered on the board so the guy using it looks straight down at it during a swim, not off to one side or the other. Using it is an art—some guys are wonderful with it, others never seem to get the hang of it."

Depth gauges are off-the-shelf models designed for sport and commercial diving. They are remarkably accurate, typically good to about 18 meters. It is used for both navigation and safety. You can, for example, judge the distance from where you are under water to the high water mark if you know the slope of the bottom on a particular beach; the 10ft line on the chart might be 50m from the high water line. Once you find that 10ft depth on the bottom you have a pretty accurate idea of just how far you have to go.

The depth gauge has a critical safety function when you're on oxygen. The Draegers work well in shallow water, but breathing straight oxygen below 35ft quickly poisons the body. Without the depth gauge, it is quite easy to drift down past that level, with possibly fatal consequences.

While most attack boards are rigged to accept a light stick for illumination, most SEALs think that even this weak glow is far too bright for security. Instead, most just use the luminous markings on the compass, clock and depth gauge. "Even that luminescence is visible from the surface in real clear water," a SEAL says, "and we worry about it when we get in around piers, where it could be seen by a sentry."

The watch itself is a standard item, but it is important to have it on the board, rather than on the wrist of the swimmer. That's because stability and consistency are so important on an underwater swim; you don't want the navigator looking down at his wrist every few minutes because it will invariably throw him off course a bit.

Navigating accurately under water is one of the most challenging things for SEALs to learn, but some become extremely adept at the skill. Each SEAL learns how far each kick propels him through the water; by counting kicks he can calculate how far he has traveled. It works so well that some SEALs can swim long distances (up to 3mi) and surface within just 5m of their intended objective.

Dive Knife

SEALs have gone through dozens of different knife designs during the fifty years since the UDT days. The orig-

Attack Board

The attack board, or compass board is a very simple device with an extremely important function; it is the basic tool for navigating during sub-surface combat swims. In fact, on normal operations, the only thing visible under water will be the luminous dials of the compass, depth

Detail, SOMAV assault vest. A vest or H harness is the foundation for "Line 2" equipment, the place where grenades, magazines, canteens, small radios, and survival gear gets stashed. The SOMAV version is especially good at preventing magazines from falling out at inopportune times, just one example of the attention to detail that goes into everything associated with SEAL operations.

inal versions were either standard issue fighting knives or bayonets—they were all that was available. A special UDT design, adapted to a salt water working environment, came along in the 1950s. That knife was replaced by the legendary Kaybar, long a favorite of SEALs and many others in all the armed forces. By the 1960s many sport dive knives and fighting knives were available commercially as off-the-shelf items; SEALs bought them out of their own pockets—for real and imagined virtues.

Others simply used gear from the dive locker or the supply room. "I used the bayonet for the M-16," says one. "I sharpened it really well, it was pointy, and if I ever needed to, I could put it on the end of my M-16 for extra reach in a fight." But $150 Randall knives were also popular, and some SEALs swore by them.

Then the community went looking for a standard knife that met the basic requirements of the mission that could be issued to everybody. The result was a huge, heavy, over-engineered Buck knife that was pretty good for banging on the

Attack board. Normally this tool will have a depth gauge and watch attached, besides the compass. The swimmer watches the compass constantly on the dive. By swimming in a consistent way, counting each kick, you can judge with fair accuracy how far you've traveled. It is just one of the many martial arts BUD/S students learn in training, and perfect on the teams.

hull of a submarine to let the crew know you want back in—and for presenting to VIPs, which has become its principal application.

"I have yet to meet anybody in our community who has ever cut a throat," says Gary Stubblefield. "We use them to cut wire, we use them to open C-ration cans, and we bang on the hulls of submarines with the hilt. But I don't know of anybody who's ever done anything nefarious with one. I don't want to use one to fight with somebody—why not do that with a bullet? Don't bring a knife to a gunfight."

Watch

SEALs were once issued fancy, very expensive dive watches at government expense, but no more. There are plenty of good, durable, accurate—and cheap—dive watches for sale at every K-Mart. The basic criteria for SEAL use is that a watch must be water-proof to reasonable depth, shock-proof, accurate, and subdued in appearance. One of the best is the Casio G-Shock model, a standard digital watch in a rubberized housing.

One of the real problems with all watches is reading them at night. Even the faint light used to illuminate the digital models can be seen at a great distance; so, too, can the luminous hands of a traditional analogue design. Both have given away the position of patrols in both training and real-world ops so SEALs and most other people in combatant units buy covers for their watch faces. It is the kind of attention to tiny detail that can keep you alive or get you shot.

Slate

One of the most important items of equipment for hydrographic recon missions is also one of the most simple and inexpensive, a piece of Plexiglas called a slate. Instead of a grease pencil, the slate is used with a common lead pencil on the end of a short lanyard. Once the surface is roughened with sandpaper it is quite easy to write upon, and the lead pencil won't smear as readily. The slate is extremely useful for many applications, including taking notes out in the woods.

The durable, cheap, reliable plastic slate, though, is being targeted for replacement by tiny battery powered recording devices that are likely to be more accurate and easier to use—until the batteries wear out in the middle of a mission.

The slate is likely to be around for a while, at least for the beach survey mission, but even that will probably be modernized with a combination GPS, recorder, and depth-finder someday.

Grenades & Pyrotechnics
M-67 Frag

The standard M-67 "baseball" grenade is an anti-personnel weapon that doesn't get used very much on real-world ops anymore. A lot of M-67s were thrown around Southeast Asia, though, twenty years ago, and it proved to be a useful tool in the SEAL bag of tricks.

The grenade is not much more that a round sheet metal container with a length of notched wire and a small quantity of explosive inside and a fuse assembly on top. Once you pull the pin and toss the thing (allowing the "spoon" to fly off, igniting the fuse train) there will be about a 6-second interlude before the grenade goes off. It is a good idea to toss the thing at least 45ft because anything inside that distance stands a good chance of getting a hurt. It is also a good idea to avoid having the thing bounce off tree limbs overhead and bounce back at you—which happens all too often.

Grenades, in fact, are dangerous. A lot of Americans have been hurt and killed by their own grenades; they straighten the pins, for instance, which then work loose unexpectedly, firing the grenade. Sometimes the bad guys catch them, too, and throw them back. If somebody on your squad makes a weak toss, the grenade can land at your feet.

So SEALs carry grenades very carefully; instead of hooking the spoons on your LBE, you carry them in a magazine pouch or a canteen cover on your pistol belt. It doesn't look as cool, but they are almost as accessible and a lot better protected. And instead of straightening the pins, you use 1in masking tape to secure the ring. It adds a little resistance to

The Mk 138 satchel charge. The bag contains ten blocks of explosive, a time fuse, an M-60 fuse lighter, and det cord. A bladder and oral inflation tube allows you to neutralize the buoyancy of the package, making it easier to swim with.

the pull, but—as one SEAL says, "you'd be amazed how strong you get when you are in a state of abject terror."

M18 Claymore

The M-16 Claymore revolutionized and transformed the American conduct of ambushes and of defensive positions when it first was issued back in the 1960s. It is an elegantly simple weapon, not much more that a pound of C4 explosives and 100 steel ball bearings in a plastic case. But when fired, the Claymore sprays those steel balls in a wide fan that will kill or wound every man in a squad or rip a gaping hole in a human wave attack coming through the wire of your compound.

Normally, the M-18 is fired electrically with an electrical blasting cap, a 100m length of wire, and a hand-held firing device. SEALs in Viet Nam, though, learned to carry one rigged with a 10-second time fuse and a fuse lighter; when the bad guys were in hot pursuit down the trail all you had to do was pull out the Claymore, prop it up and pop the fuse lighter—then run like hell. If your timing was good, the bad guys would come hopping down the bunny trail about the time the 10 seconds expired—a guaranteed method for discouraging anybody from following you further. Now, of course, that lesson is forgotten and SEALs are not permitted to train in the use of this technique, or even be instructed in its use... because it isn't safe, say the headquarters pukes.

Light Sticks

Among the many little technical improvements in military equipment today are the little tubes of chemical compounds called light sticks. Within the flexible plastic tube is a small glass ampoule; when the stick is bent, the glass ampoule breaks and the two compounds mix. The result is a soft glowing light that lasts for hours.

All the armed forces—especially the SEALs—have found dozens of applications for these disposable devices. Put a few of these things on a rubber duck for a night jump into the middle of the ocean and you can probably find the boat once you are in the water. If you and all the members of the squad attach one to your web gear, link-up in the dark water will be far easier. If security is a real problem and you're worried about attracting the wrong kind of attention, the light sticks can be attached to the SEAL with a lanyard and only activated if there is a problem.

Such a problem occurred during Operation Urgent Fury, before the devices were in wide distribution. A squad made a night parachute insertion to the water off Grenada—without the light sticks or any beacons or link-up aids. Not only did one of the two boats drift away, and several SEALs drown—even worse, the mission wasn't completed.

"They became so good that we started using them for everything; we put them on attack boards, use them for little night lights, and marking landing zones for helicopters. You can even hang them on a weighted line from a helicopter when you are descending toward the surface at night, when it is very difficult to judge how high off the deck you are. But you know immediately when the light stick hits the surface."

The sticks come in many colors, and there's even an infrared version that is almost invisible to the eye but that shows up like a bright beacon when viewed with a thermal imaging device.

LBE & Vests

Like the Army's Rangers, Special Forces, infantry units, and Marine Corps rifle companies, SEALs have a close-quarter battle mission that requires some special personal equipment. For SEALs this is "Line Two" gear, the essentials

A Heckler & Koch P7 9mm pistol. A favorite of many on the teams, the H&K accepts a silencer quite readily. "Silencer" is a bit of a misnomer—sound suppresser is more accurate. But H&K MP5s and P7s are nearly silent when used with subsonic ammunition; then, when you fire, the only sound is a quiet little putt, the sound of the weapon chambering another round, and the sound a bullet makes when it strikes its target.

for combat, and it is worn on the chest in either an "H-harness" or a custom-brewed Ranger-style vest.

About three out of four SEALs will use the Navy-issue H-harness, called Load-Bearing Equipment (LBE) by the Army and Marine Corps. Its foundation is a 3in wide pistol belt, supported by a set of sturdy suspenders. On this foundation, attached by metal clips, are added magazine pouches, canteens, knife scabbards and pistol holsters. The suspenders normally have a "blow-out patch" battle dressing on one shoulder, a strobe light in a pouch on the other. Extra canteen covers may be installed, but not for water; SEALs discovered long ago that they make superb containers for M-16 magazines and for grenades. The clips work loose, sometimes unnoticed, so most SEALs use parachute suspension line (called 550 cord, or "dummy cord") to secure each item.

Often, but not always installed on vests and harness, will be a rock-climber's carabinier ("beener" in the vernacular), generally on the right front shoulder. The beener is used in rappelling and for SPIE rig helicopter extractions as an essential safety device but serves as a handy place to stow all sorts of things, like gloves, that need to be accessible in a hurry.

A lot of SEALs invest in commercial assault vests, investing several hundred dollars in each. There are some virtues to this concept of an integral system—without all those unreliable metal clips. The Army has developed one and issued the design to some specialized units. Back in 1986, SPECWARCOM's RDT&E staff contracted with a company called SOMAV to build a vest specifically for the needs of

NSW. The prototypes were issued to one of the platoons in ST3; after a couple of months the platoon came back with a list of modifications needed. Those changes were incorporated and the modified design again sent to the field for practical testing; a few more changes resulted.

The final product is a unique design that is remarkably efficient; it incorporates horizontal magazine pouches that are easily opened and secured with one hand (a modern miracle). Each pouch holds two 30-round mags, but in a way that lets you remove one without having the other fall out at the same time. The vest also provides for an integral flotation bladder, removable for desert operations. The fit is adjustable for each individual, unlike the H-harness, helping to insure no rattles. After the final fine-tuning, the design was presented to the Navy—which declined to buy any. But SPECWARCOM found a few dollars somewhere and sixty or seventy of the vests built for the teams.

Even loaded up with magazines, water, flashlights, radios, and the other fashion accessories well-dressed SEALs wear to a party, these harnesses and vests are surprisingly comfortable. You can run and move quite well in the gear, considering the load, if you've set up the harness or vest properly. And it better be comfortable, too, because it will probably not come off for the duration of the entire mission, unless it is a particularly long one. If the team gets compromised, if you have to make a run for the beach, you might ditch your ruck but you better not discard your weapon or your Line Two gear. And if you have the poor judgment to let yourself get shot, your swim buddy can drag you out of the line of fire by grabbing the back of the harness, between the shoulder blades, and using it as a handle for you. It is a very good system, but there are very few of those SOMAV rigs left on the teams.

Two limpet mines attached to a swimmer harness. On the beach, they are heavy and awkward to maneuver or carry long distances. In the water, though, the mines are neutrally buoyant and easy to handle. Visible, facing the camera, are the receptacles for the priming mechanism and its timer assembly.

Chapter Four

Insertion and Extraction Techniques

SEAL operations are obviously hazardous, but the most critical parts of special operations, the most hazardous moments of all, tend to be getting in and out of the operational area—inserting and extracting. If you are going to get whacked, it will most likely happen at these two times.

But SEALs have some advantages over Green Berets and Rangers; despite the challenges of long ocean transits in rubber ducks, or lock out/lock in submarine procedures, the water provides a kind of armor for SEALs that isn't available to the Army's special operators, or the conventional forces of all the combatant formations. It's a mighty big ocean to hide in, and no enemy can defend an entire coast line. After fifty years of combat swimming, the Navy has polished and refined its insertion and extraction techniques to a fine military art. Here's how they do it:

First, there are a lot of choices:

• You can ride a small boat in from over the horizon; a small boat with a minimal radar signature can easily disappear into the "sea clutter" on a radar screen. Depending on the kind of boat, you can disappear into the routine offshore vessel traffic, looking like an innocent fishing boat, a pleasure craft, a small freighter, a dhow, a barge, a sampan. A black Combat Rubber Raiding Craft won't blend into this traffic, but if you execute in the middle of the night, you and the little boat will just blend into the water, and that's good enough. All have proved successful in the recent past.

• You can launch from a submarine close inshore, with or without a CRRC. If the sub can get in to 600 to 1000

Left: Fast roping from a Pave Hawk version of the SH-60, a squad deploys to a barge.

Right: A SEAL assumes the "prepare to land" position about 100ft above the water. He has turned the MC1-1 canopy into the wind—its 5 knot forward speed will compensate for the light breeze blowing, essentially stopping forward motion directly over the place he wants to enter the water.

'Of all my combat operations in Viet Nam, only two were dry— all the rest involved getting off the boat and into the water or mud.'

Tied to the pier at Ft. Everglades, Florida, the USS James Polk provides a rare glimpse of the dry deck shelter used by SEALs and the SDV. The Polk is a "nukie" and a dedicated SEAL support platform. U.S. Navy

meters to the beach, you will probably dispense with the rubber duck and just swim in. Such a mission will give the sub crew heart failure, but that's their problem.

• You can launch from a sub well offshore, 5 miles or more, (which will only give the submariners indigestion) if you have the use of a SEAL Delivery Vehicle (SDV). The SDV is a miniature sub that can cruise along under water at four or five knots; it will take two swim pairs—a fire team—well in shore, completely submerged. The technique is so good that the SDV was used a lot in the Gulf—and we can't tell you more than that.

• You can jump in, either on shore or into the water, using any of three basic combat parachute insertion techniques—static line, HAHO (high altitude jump, high altitude 'chute opening), or HALO (high altitude jump,

way to get a squad or platoon aboard a ship or an oil platform; there is nothing surreptitious about it, but there are times when stealth isn't important at all and surprise and shock are essential. Helicopter insertions, done right, are stunningly powerful.

• Or, as was SOP in Viet Nam, you can ride a PBR, RIB, MATC, or PBL up to the shoreline, jump over the side, and get stuck in the mud.

All of these methods, properly executed, should deliver you to the beach and from there on, you work whatever magic the team has been assigned for its mission. Then it is time to, as they say, get the heck out of Dodge.

The same techniques you used to get in work just as well coming out—but try to avoid doing the same thing both times. The opposing team might have missed your arrival out on Pier 32, but after the charges detonate they will probably put two and two together—and will be studying your footprints carefully. Pier 32 will not be a good place to visit for some time. So you ought to find both another place and a different technique for extraction. If the enemy thinks, for example, that you've come in with the help of a submarine, they will probably throw every patrol craft they've got into the search for your pasty, overfed, submariner pals waiting impatiently like the fat target they are in shallow water off the beach. Of course, if you've set the clock fuse timers for enough delay you can get back aboard and underway before the C4 goes off, but that's not always possible. So here is what one team commander has to say about extractions:

"We have a couple of rules we try to follow; one is, we go in and come out different ways or routes if we can. We might swim in with the Draegers, but come out with a helicopter or a boat. If we have already revealed ourselves to the enemy then concealment is a lot less important than speed. We have learned the hard way, at the cost of men's lives, that if we go in and come out the same way, somebody's going to set up an ambush on us.

"When you insert, you go from a known point to a known point. Going back it is more difficult; there is no X marked out there on the water where the sub will be waiting and until GPS that was a guessing game. The sub has only a small time window where he can wait for you, and finding him without GPS and beacons was a real tough problem.

"When we start thinking about detection, the first thing you have to worry about is the 'Mk 1 Mod Zero Eyeball,' which has always been very good at finding us. It is limited by things like fog and night, but with night vision devices that limitation is decreased. We also have to worry about infrared sensors, but thermal sensors are even more of a worry. Very inexpensive thermal sensors are on the market now that can pick up a guy in the water, or the heat from an outboard engine at tremendous ranges. So when you plan an operation and make your decision on how you are going to insert and extract, you've got to include in your calculations your best information about what kinds of systems will

low altitude 'chute opening). If you use the conservative, tried-and-true static line method, you can bring your boat with you. If you use HALO or HAHO, you can fly yourself for many miles through the nighttime sky from the point where you stepped out of the aircraft, arriving silently and with great precision—on top of the enemy's command bunker, if that's your target.

• A helicopter can drop you off, either by landing (or hovering 10ft off the deck, more likely), rappelling, or fast-roping from 50ft or so. Fast rope is a lightning fast

A beach survey team goes over the side in a technique developed during World War II. U.S. Navy

Right: When it is time for the beach survey team to come back with the scoop, the recovery is a reverse of the insertion. They form a long line, with swimmers about 50 yards apart. As the boat comes roaring along the line, each swimmer reaches up and snags the rubber loop at the end of a big bungee cord, to be jerked out of the water and into the boat. U.S. Navy

be operating against you—and always assuming a worst-case scenario. The whole thing is getting more difficult because even third-world nations are acquiring excellent sensor systems now."

Small Boat Insertions—
Special Boat Unit Combatant Craft

Despite all the training for exotic insertion and extraction techniques with SDVs and subs, perhaps ninety percent of all ops in the real world involve boat rides. During the war in Viet Nam, the boats were usually fast boats designed for the job. It was, and is, a dangerous, difficult mission just to get the team to the front door of the operational area. In a riverine or intercoastal environment the boat will be in range of almost every weapon. You can get hit anywhere, and if you do these insertions for long you certainly will get hit.

"You don't get to relax on the way in—it isn't a bus ride. The boat crew will make several false insertions—nosing into the bank, pretending to put you ashore—then pull back and move on up the river. The team has to be wide awake, locked and loaded, because the enemy will try to open up on you when the boat is a fat, slow target turning into the shoreline. It is the most vulnerable time, and the boat captain will expose the boat this way half a dozen times just making the insertion. VC units became adept at anticipating possible SEAL insertion locations, then set up ambushes on them; lots of teams and boat crews fought it out, toe-to-toe, before the operations ever began."

The security team may wait and watch for some time, looking for sentries or other activity on the beach or inland.

Right and next page: Once the beach seems clear, the security swimmers move in to the beach, remove fins (securing them to lanyards) and check weapons for sand. They cover the beach while the vulnerable RIB comes ashore. Robert Genet

The boats will try to get the team onto the bank with dry feet—but it probably won't happen. As one SEAL says, "Of all my sixty-five real-world combat operations in Viet Nam, only two were dry—all the rest involved getting off the boat and into the water or mud. Getting in is *always* an ordeal."

Submarine Lock out/Lock in

Launching out of a submarine is an ordeal, too, wet or dry. The "nukies" are crowded, with little space for the team. There are never enough bunks for everybody, so you "hot bunk," or trade with somebody else who works while you sleep, who sleeps while you work. Then there is the problem of claustrophobia; the sub itself is bad, but the lock in/lock out chamber induces panic even among some SEALs. "It's just a teeny space, an air bubble and some water. I have been in there with guys who just panicked; it's that tight."

Once the chamber hatch opens there are several ways to get to the surface and back. One is the "breath hold" technique; you just hold your breath and swim to the surface. If you do this, remember to gradually exhale during the whole ascent, otherwise your lungs will explode.

Another technique involves "open circuit" SCUBA tanks—the safest method for the diver but objectionable

to the sub crew because of the noise of the bubbles, a "signature" that makes the sub a target to any nearby alert adversary with modern detection technology.

Finally, there is the Draeger—which can be dangerous since its maximum safe operational depth is only about 35ft.

Then there is the problem of available equipment. Even with a CRRC stowed in an exterior locker, getting the rubber duck deployed and recovered is a nightmare. Real-world operations won't usually bother with recovering the boat and motor, but during training these inflatables have to be deflated and dragged down to be folded, lashed, and secured back in the locker forward of the sub's sail.

Loading and launching the boat is yet another nightmare; there will be wind and current pushing and pulling the sub and the rubber boat, towed by the sub at the end of the ascent line. The SEALs have to swim up the ascent line, clamber aboard the boat with their gear, then huddle in the wind while the rest of the team come out through the chamber,

Bottom: A UDT frogman detonates demolition charges attached to underwater obstacles while the amphibious ship awaits on the horizon to commence the landing as soon as the area is cleared. US Navy

Here's a look at a subsurface swim with an attack board. U.S. Navy

Above: Twin dry deck shelters on the deck of a sub. The dry deck shelter (DDS) is a huge improvement on the lockout chamber. U.S. Navy

Bottom: Launching an SDV. U.S. Navy

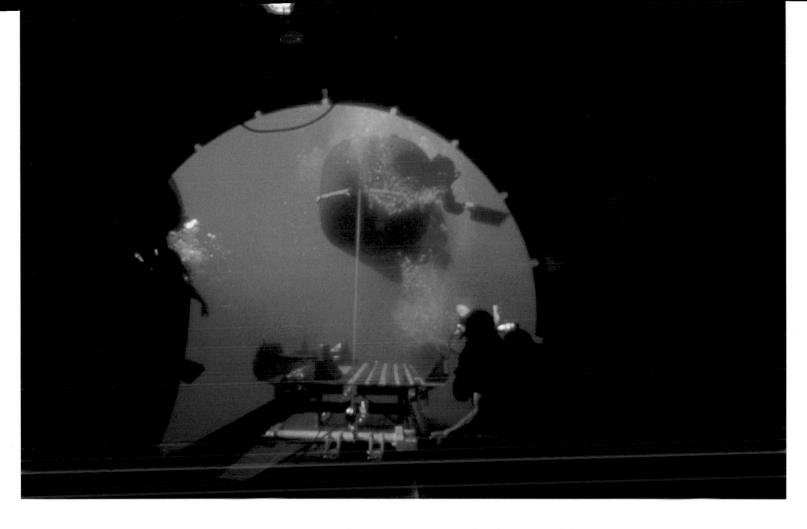

Above: The DDS is only dry if you keep the hatch secured. Here's the view from inside during launch of an SDV. U.S. Navy

Bottom: Another successful SDV launch. U.S. Navy

three at a time, and up to the surface. Unless the sub crew is very experienced at all this, they may take a "depth excursion," towing the boat and its crew back under water. This is not conducive to a smooth insertion. No matter what the climate, the people in the boat will probably be freezing.

The motor for the boat is a special one, modified and prepared for immersion. Even so, salt water is hard on equipment and getting the engine "lit off" can be a challenge—or an impossibility.

"Submarines are nice for getting into an area, but they are a nightmare to work out of!" says one veteran SEAL.

SEAL Delivery Vehicle

The SDV is equally challenging, although nobody makes it to the surface. But both the vehicle and the SEALs have to be launched from the sub, and the SDV hangs on its tether for long minutes while everybody gets the pieces of the puzzle together. Two SEALs crew

the SDV while another four ride in back. All breathe air from open-circuit systems installed on the SDV.

It is a cold, black ride into the delivery point. Nobody—not even the SDV pilot or navigator up front— can see out. Navigation is entirely on instruments, with inertial guidance technology indicating position; sonar and other sensors provide obstacle avoidance and beacons help the SDV and sub rendezvous.

It is a cold, cramped, boring ride. At least when you're swimming your activity generates some heat but even 80-degree water will gradually drain your body's heat. There isn't much to look at. You can, at least, chat with the other guys; the masks worn on the SDV permit speech.

Despite all the drawback, SDVs got a good workout in the Persian Gulf. Doing what, you ask? Sorry, those missions are still classified—but the folks who did them have a smirking, satisfied little grin when they decline to describe just what happened.

A DDS crew takes time during a training mission to pose for an underwater portrait. US Navy

Bottom: The DDS hangar supervisor monitors the deck crewmen as they wrestle the SDV down onto the DDS cradle for recovery. US Navy

The DDS deck captain relays final navigational information to the SDV navigator prior to a launch from the DDS. US Navy

Fast Rope

Fast rope is the insertion method of choice from a helicopter, unless you can somehow put the aircraft on the deck and let people jump out. You can come in fully loaded, from 90ft above the deck of a ship, a roof, a bunker, or oil platform—sliding right past all those masts and antennas (hopefully). It takes just a few seconds to deposit a whole helicopter-load of SEALs on top of a startled, confused enemy position.

Here's how you do it: the rope is a heavy, 2in line rigged from the helicopter hoist bracket. You take a good door position, reach out, firmly grasp the rope with both hands (encased in heavy leather welder's gloves) and slide. You essentially fall for about 60ft, then apply braking pressure with your gloved hands. The rope needs to be still new and still rough for best braking—and you need to have a powerful grip and excellent upper body strength. If your timing is good you will come to a screeching halt just as your toes touch the deck—throw away the gloves and dash off to your assigned mission. If your timing is poor you will splatter on the deck and then somebody else will have to do your job for you. It is very important to get out, away from the rope as soon as you're down because people are right behind you, coming down fast.

"You either do it or you don't. I know some guys who get real nervous about fast roping. I'm nervous about it in training, but less so on a real op. Then you just reach out and go, hit the deck and move on. It isn't that tough to control your speed if you aren't too heavily loaded—fifty pounds of gear, say. More than that might really drive you down harder."

Parachute

Parachute operations really look like fun during demonstrations, like the annual July 4th show at Coronado, but out in the cold, cruel world of real-life ops, jumps are a great way to get people killed. "I have a philosophy about parachute operations," a former SEAL team commander says. "Don't consider using it unless there really isn't any alternative—and then seriously question whether you should do the op at all."

A SEAL swimmer descends to the DDS during swimmer lock in/lock out operations. US Navy

That attitude is due in part to the fiasco off the coast of Grenada prior to the launch of Urgent Fury when three SEALs drowned, one of two Boston Whalers disappeared, and the mission aborted without anything being accomplished at all.

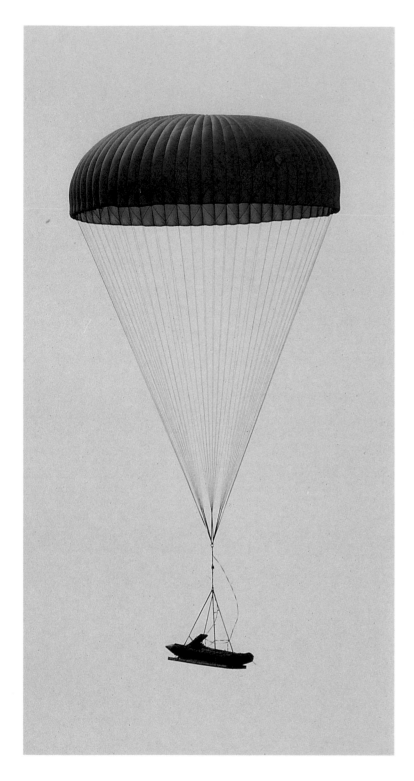

A RIB heads toward the ocean under a 100ft cargo canopy. While the canopies are pretty reliable, they occasionally fail, sometimes dramatically. Parachute drops are among the riskiest military operations—not because the chutes fail, but because they deliver people and equipment in ways that are very difficult to control.

Right: Watch out for that first step—it's about 10,000ft. A free-fall parachutist launches himself into space. U.S. Navy

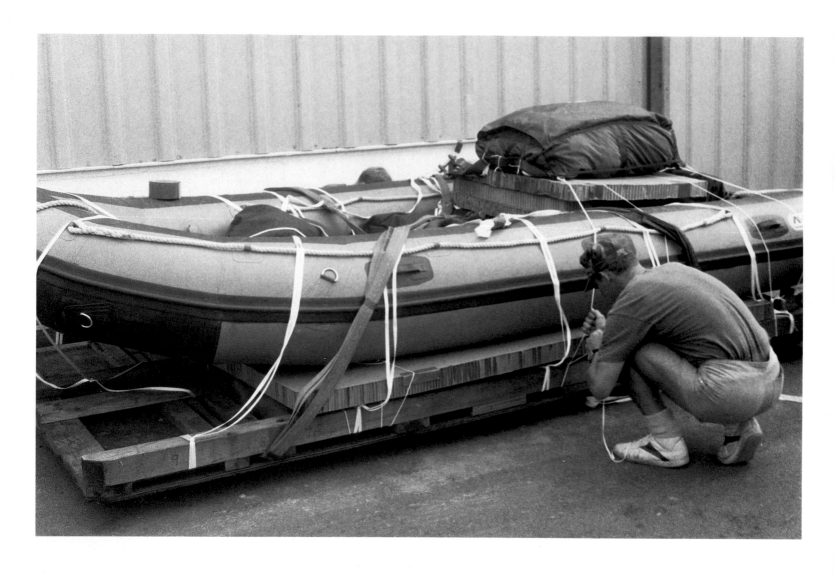

The riggers are just about done prepping the boat for its big adventure. It will slide out the back of a C-130, pulled by a drogue/pilot 'chute, followed immediately by its crew. Once all are safely down, the SEALs have to extricate the boat from all the lines and the canopy before they can ride off to the objective. U.S. Navy

Next page top: The preferred method of departure from the scene of the crime is to have the helo actually land and let you climb aboard.

Next page bottom: SEALs call it "helo-casting" and the preferred method is to have the helicopter fly at 30 knots, 30ft off the water; hold on to your mask, say your prayers, and go! If the pilot is a little sloppy at this you may find yourself creaming in at fifty knots from 50ft—a good way to break bones and lose equipment, and it happens. U.S. Navy

Air drops of boats look so clean and simple, but it takes plenty of equipment and prep time to make the drop work. Here are the supplies required to drop a single 24ft RIB: 100ft cargo parachute, tie-down straps, shock-absorbing material, breakaway cord, shackles, and buoys. In combat it is all disposable—but in training you'd better bring it all back to the riggers in the para loft. U.S. Navy

SPIE rigging. It is a fun, breezy ride, with a good safety record.

While SPIE rigging and helicopter rides may look dramatic and glamorous, the traditional method is to stagger back aboard a boat, soaking wet, covered with mud, oozing blood here and there, and exhausted to the core.

Previous page top: Get me outta here! These SEALs are about to get a real "E-ticket" ride underneath a Navy helicopter, an extraction technique called SPIE rigging. Charles Mussi/Foto Consortium

Previous page bottom: Helicopter support for SEAL ops has improved tremendously over the years. Instead of bare-bones Hueys, as in Viet Nam, SEALs can call for the NSW battlefield taxi, the powerful and extremely capable special ops version of the SH-60 Sea Hawk. With twin 7.62mm machine guns, night vision capability, and enough power to pull a bull moose through a tuba, this marvelous chopper has a reputation among its crews and the teams as a "lead sled," able to fly away with anything you can stuff inside.

An alternate method for getting the heck out of Dodge is to climb back aboard, up a ladder. That is a long, hard climb when all your gear is soaking and you've absorbed a bullet or some shrapnel but it beats the alternative.

No matter how big a lunk the guy is, you have to bring his carcass home. SEALs never leave another SEAL on the battlefield, living or dead. Charles Mussi/Foto Consortium

Although a squad isn't really much of a major maneuver element in the grand art of land warfare, there are some times and places where SEALs might have to charge up the hill and take a position. This squad demonstrates how it is done: one fire team (the base element), at top, takes up firing positions and places a high volume of aimed fire on the enemy position. The other half, the maneuver element, assaults forward in a rapid bounding movement, then takes up firing positions. Now the roles will swap, and the two fire teams will leap-frog forward, applying relentless pressure on the defenders. Charles Mussi/Foto Consortium

One of the things a SEAL squad really likes to avoid is an actual shooting contest with an enemy force. That's because the opposing team tends to outnumber our merry band of heroes about 100 to one; no matter how bad they are as marksmen, a stray round is likely to catch somebody sooner or later. So these SEALs from Group Two add a little realism to their training by adding a casualty. Charles Mussi/Foto Consortium

SEALs tend to minimize the amount of food carried on operations, often doing without unless the op lasts more than 24 hours. This one, though, is digging into an MRE entree, the standard combat ration. There are twelve variations, all quite good—until you've had them every day for a week or two. Robert Genat/Zone Five Photo

Right: This SEAL sniper has taken up a hasty position. Ordinarily, given time, the sniper team literally disappears from view. You can stand right on top of their "hide" and not know of their presence. Robert Genat/Zone Five Photo

Chapter Five

Things That Go Bump in the Night—An Overview

Wanna know a military secret? Explosives are fun! Demolition materials are extremely useful for all sorts of things, most are quite safe to handle, and, as one Marine says, "there are very few of life's problems that can't be solved with high explosives!"

SEALs, over the years, have used incredible quantities of TNT and C4, hundreds of miles of detonating cord, and tens of thousands of blasting caps. In the process, countless beach obstacles have been destroyed, bridges dropped, ships and boats sunk, and railroad trains derailed.

Tools of the Trade
Limpet Mine

A very small quantity of explosives placed in a vulnerable spot can do an amazing amount of damage. That is the idea behind the limpet mine. Current models aren't a whole lot different than those used during World War II and are delivered pretty much the same way, with a sub-surface swim.

The device is designed to be carried on the back of the swimmer, attached with a simple harness. Once under the target, the harness is removed, the mine's magnets pried from the steel plate that has held each in position, then placed next to the steel hull of the vessel. A mechanical clock timer provides up to two and a half hours for a getaway.

The mine actually contains very little explosive, but it is designed as a shaped charge to focus and magnify the power of the detonation. One limpet by itself will probably not sink a modern warship, all of which are designed to tolerate some battle damage below the

Three and a half pounds of fertilizer/fuel oil mix make an impressive bang. While not terribly powerful, the stuff is easy to make, cheap, and excellent for certain applications.

Right: "Hmmmm... a few well-placed and well-timed explosives here could flush out the enemy and seal off a possible escape route. Yeah, why not?"

Fire in the Hole

A Short Course in Military Explosives

As one Marine says, 'There are very few of life's problems that can't be solved with high explosives!'

Yikes—do we really have to poke a spike in that stick of dynamite? Yes, we do, and it is perfectly safe. Dynamite won't detonate without a very sharp jolt from det cord or a blasting cap; this stick is being primed with a section of det cord.

waterline, but it will certainly produce a substantial hole in the hull of even the biggest carrier. That damage will degrade the ability of the ship to function, possibly prevent it from getting underway. Several limpets, strategically placed, can break the keel of any ship and may very well send the biggest to the bottom.

Mk 138 Satchel Charge

Satchel charges became essential tools for assaulting defended positions early in World War II—simple, nearly foolproof, systems for eliminating all kinds of problems in the surf zone, on the beach, or in the hinterland beyond. Today's Mk 138 version is almost identical to the same device used half a century ago: a simple canvas shoulder bag with about 40lb of explosive, primed with a non-electric blasting cap on the end of a section of time fuse. The time fuse is pre-cut to a reasonably short delay, determined by the mission. An M-60 waterproof fuse lighter makes it easy to get things started; all you've got to do is prop the satchel up against the side of the enemy bunker or obstruction, pull the pin on the fuse lighter, and make your exit.

A military time fuse. While not quite as reliable as electrical circuits, time fuse is much more practical for shots on operations, where the team wants to be far, far away with the charges detonate.

Right: Here's one stick of dynamite—not much of a bang, not enough power to do much damage. Dynamite is useful for the same kinds of projects as nitrate/fuel oil mix, deliberate engineering applications rather than in combat. SEALs use it, though, for many projects.

C4

Plastic explosive comes in many formulations but the variety called C4 has been an American military mainstay for many years. It is a white solid material that looks just like stiff window putty or modeling clay. It is easy to mold into any shape. Like many modern explosives, it is quite stable and insensitive. That means it is safe to store and handle until it is primed with a cap or other initiating material. Green Berets in Viet Nam commonly used

A non-electric blasting cap. A simple metal tube half-filled with an extremely powerful and sensitive explosive, the cap is probably the most dangerous thing a blaster handles.

Det cord looks almost exactly like time fuse, but lacks the yellow band. But while time fuse burns at about 40sec to the foot, det cord explodes at about 5 miles per second! Det cord is used to tie charges together, detonating all of them at virtually the same instant.

bits of the stuff as fuel to heat C-rations. SEALs used it by the ton to blow VC bunkers and tunnel complexes. It is the modern military blasting material of choice.

Time Fuse

Although blasters generally prefer firing shots electrically, there are certainly many times when M700 time fuse works best. The material is quite simple and has been around for many years. It is no more than a bit of black powder encased in a reinforced green plastic tube with yellow bands every 72in or 90in. The material is only about 1/5in in diameter and is waterproof. It typically burns at the rate of forty seconds per foot—although you must test each length before use and anything faster than thirty seconds to the foot will require another batch of fuse.

Fuse is only good for one thing, initiating a standard non-electric blasting cap. No other modern military explosive will react to it, although in the distant past

charges using blasting powder (coarse black powder) could be fired with fuse.

You prime a charge with it this way: first, cut and discard about 6in from one end to eliminate any possibility of moisture contamination. The cut should be square and clean. Calculate the delay, based on the actual burning rate of the fuse, then cut exactly that length. With the charges already prepared and (hopefully) positioned, you gently place the fuse into the well of a standard M-7 blasting cap, seating it on the ferrule inside; don't force

Crimping the cap to the time fuse must be done with a measured hand. The amount of explosive inside isn't great, but it is powerful enough to maim a hand.

Previous page top: An M-60 fuse lighter. This simple device works under water or out in the jungle with excellent reliability. Just remove the safety pin, pull back the spring-loaded firing pin, and release. A primer lights the fuse—then it is time to leave. Note the small amount of smoke pouring from the plunger, a visible way to confirm that the fuse is actually burning. During training and engineering projects it is standard procedure to shout "FIRE IN THE HOLE!" three times before lighting the fuse; during combat ops in enemy territory it is standard procedure to keep your mouth shut tight.

Previous page bottom: The official name for this little electrical generator is M57 Firing Device, but everybody calls it a "clacker." One squeeze will fire an electrical blasting cap at the end of a 100ft wire.

This is about half a pound of C4, ready to prime. This is really handy stuff—safe to handle, easy to shape, powerful, and stable in long-term storage.

it! Then, with the crimping portion of the tool, prepare to crimp the cap on the fuse—but, before applying pressure, raise your hands and the materials overhead, then gently crimp the cap. If the cap detonates now you will only loose your fingers or hands, not your face.

Now the cap can be inserted in the well of a block of TNT or into a pocket punched in C4 or dynamite. The cap and fuse assembly then is secured with a priming adapter and usually with electrical tape or twine. Finally, you are almost ready to fire the shot.

Fuse Lighter

Time fuse can be lit with a match; you split it with a knife, put the head in the slit, then strike the match. But

Primadet is a relatively new development, a very reliable priming system that combines the virtues of det cord with some of the procedures of electrical circuits. The orange cord is actually a tiny, safe version of det cord, fired with a shotgun-like primer. It avoids the vices of both time fuse and electrical circuits; SEALs like it a lot.

Special operators prepare to do a little body and fender work on a pre-owned vehicle recently owned by the Iraqi army.
U.S. Navy

that tends to attract attention at night, especially in the bad sort of neighborhoods frequented by operators, so fuse lighters are much preferred.

The M-60 fuse lighter is a simple, versatile device used by SEALs in several ways. It is a plastic housing with a shot-gun-type primer inside, fired by a spring loaded pin. It is waterproof under most conditions so you can use it under water. The end of the fuse is inserted, the collet tightened, and the device is ready to fire. If you want to light the pow-der train simply remove the safety pin—yell "fire in the hole!" three times if you are in a training situation—and then pull the plunger back, then let it go. The primer will fire with a soft "pop" and the fuse should begin to burn. You will be able to see and hear the black powder sizzling along toward the cap. Now is a good time to make a break for the exit. That is the primary use for the fuse lighter, M-60. But it is designed to be rigged with a trip wire to prime booby-traps, too.

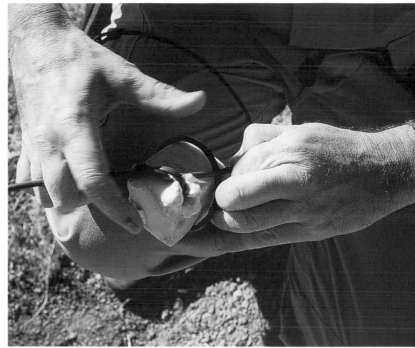

Poke a hole in the block and tie it into a length of det cord; prime the cord and you're ready to fire the shot.

turns around a block of TNT or C4 will reliably detonate the charge.

Since it explodes so fast and forcefully, det cord is used to link many charges to fire at the same moment. For example, you can bring down all the supports of a bridge together if the charges on each pier are connected to each other with a length of det cord. It works so well at this that it is issued in 500ft and 1,000ft spools.

It will also work to cut down small trees, all by itself, if you take a few turns around the tree. And, for those convoy ambush missions, you can hide lengths of the stuff in roadside ditches in the kill zone; when the

The cut end of a section of det cord reveals the explosive core.

Det Cord

Detonating cord, called "det cord" universally, is mighty interesting stuff. It looks just like time fuse—about 1/4in diameter, dark green in color. But, instead of burning at a slow, quiet rate like fuse, det cord explodes at a rate of about five *miles* per second!

Det cord is built around a thin core of a very high explosive called PETN about the thickness of a pencil lead; around this core are several layers of cotton fabric, rayon, and asphalt with a polyethylene cover. Despite the tiny amount of explosive in the cord, a couple of ambush is initiated, any survivors of your guns will dive for the protection of the ditches—which is poor protection indeed when you fire the det cord.

Dynamite

Dynamite is used by SEALs and most other military organizations, but not for strike missions. It is excellent for construction projects, engineering applications, and other deliberate work in secure areas. Dynamite, until fairly recently, used a formulation that included nitroglycerin, an extremely powerful and unstable material. Modern dynamite uses no nitro and is quite stable, much like TNT and C4. It isn't as flexible, though, for the many kinds of applications for which SEALs and other combat units use explosives, so it gets used less frequently than other materials.

TNT

TNT really revolutionized military engineering when it came into widespread use over fifty years ago. It is quite powerful, is easily handled, and is somewhat water resistant. The material comes in blocks of cast material, with a well for a blasting cap. It is a pale yellow material, about the color of butter. UDT swimmers used TNT in satchel charges assembled from several blocks of explosive, primed with a cap, fuse and fuse lighter, designed to hang from beach obstacles or pill box ventilators. Even back then, charges could be linked with det cord. TNT cleared the way for amphibious assaults across the Pacific and up and down the Normandy beaches.

Fertilizer/Fuel Oil

So what do you do when you've used up all the C4 and you've absolutely, positively, got to blow it up

An M-18 Claymore anti-personnel mine. The Claymore isn't much more than a slab of C4 behind 700 steel balls, all inside this plastic case. When fired, the result is about the same as a whole squad firing shotguns in the same general direction. The spray of steel balls will take the commitment right out of a human wave attack, the kind the VC and NVA once tried to use against SEALs and Green Berets.

overnight? Make your own explosive, of course. A simple mixture of ammonium nitrate fertilizer and diesel fuel work just fine, if you place it properly and initiate it with a booster charge and blasting cap or a hefty section of det cord.

Actually, SEALs like to use ammonium nitrate in the handy, convenient prepared package (*new! Improved! Makes unhealthy bodies eight ways!*) right off the shelf. It is used in mining almost to the exclusion of the older, traditional materials, because it is so safe, economical, and easy to handle. It is available in 50lb sacks and is just about as dangerous as 50lb of pinto beans.

Right: Here's a detailed look at the priming well of a limpet mine.

The limpet and the Mk 138 satchel charge are the two primary explosive weapons systems used by SEALs, both custom-designed for the tactical problems of subsurface combat swimmers.

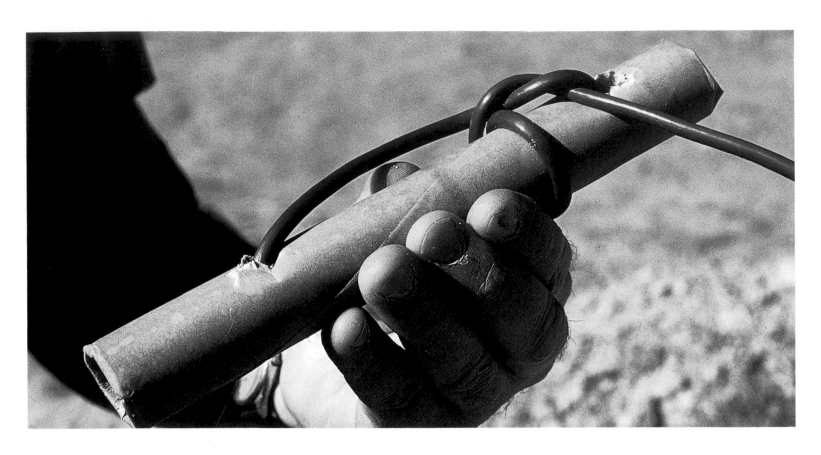

Ribbon charge is a 1/4-inch sheet of explosive backed by a strip of self-adhesive. It is easily cut to fit door locks or hinges, or for similar applications.

Previous page top: Dynamite, primed with det cord.

Previous page middle: No, not comedian Jimmy Walker's catch phrase. This really is dynamite.

Previous page bottom: C4 is popular because of characteristics such as its versatility.

Hold the onions? No, not that kind of quarter-pounder. Here's a quarter-pound block of TNT. Once the standby explosive of choice for military blasters, TNT has been largely replaced by C4.

Chapter Six

Surface Ops

Special Boat Units

'It's not the boats that are special in Special Boat units, it's the men who are special,' says a senior chief.

While the SEALs get the glory, modern Naval Special Warfare has another, essential side. Special Boat Squadrons are an integral, well-funded, currently popular component of SPECWARCOM. These squadrons, with their little rubber boats and fast little patrol craft deliver SEALs to the beach and support them by fire when they get into trouble. And even though they aren't the hulking physical specimens so often found on the teams, and although they don't go through BUD/S, be nice to them anyway—they have an attitude a lot like the pirate crews of the 18th century, but with better weapons.

"It's not the boats that are special in Special Boat units, it's the *men* who are special," says a senior chief (who asked to remain anonymous), who has been in the boats for most of a whole career. Boat crews come out of the regular fleet, but service in NSW requires a lot more from the individual and it takes somebody who likes small boats and open water to succeed in Special Boat Squadrons. Until recently the crews rotated in and out for two-year duty cycles; now the job is a career specialty with its own designator and name, *Combat Craft Crewman.* Training in the new specialty is rigorous and takes six weeks.

"You have to understand—boats are a major part of Special Warfare, too," the senior chief says. "SEALs don't

A 30ft-long RIB powers along with a small crew on board. The US Coast Guard uses these types of boats as well, and whales on theirs even harder than do the SEALs, if you can believe that. The Special Boat Squadrons use RIBs in 24ft, 30ft, and 10m (33ft) lengths.

Right: Pity the poor souls on-shore whom these eager SEALs are about to visit. The SEALs are climbing out of their Zodiac-brand inflatable to hand out some justice, SEAL style. This training maneuver is like seeing them operate with the lights on; imagine a similar landing, done silently under cover of night, carrying out their operation, and launching again with minimal noise and, ideally, no gunfire audible to enemy beyond the operation's target. Robert Genat/Zone Five Photo

Previous page: Another view of the Mk III. It was a highly successful, popular hull in its day. Each cost about a half-million dollars back in the 1970s, but they are pretty well worn out now, with cracks appearing in many places, components at the ends of their design lives, and too many little things going wrong to keep repaired. Gary Kieffer/Foto Consortium

Above: A view of the PBR Mk III, bow on. It isn't really an open ocean boat but it will do 25 knots on the rivers and bays for which it was designed. Gary Kieffer/Foto Consortium

go *anywhere* without a Special Boat detachment going along, too, because 90 percent of SEAL ops are very close to the water. But there is one thing we will go to war with most people on—we are not SEAL 'bus drivers!' Ask any SEAL who has gone to war with a boat 'det'— we take the same risks they do. If they get into trouble, we go in and get them out—under fire! During Viet Nam we had a real tight working relationship. That diminished after the war. But with all the little littoral combats we've been having, the relationship has improved again. Haiti, Panama, the Persian Gulf, Grenada—these opera-

"During Viet Nam I was attached to a Mobile Support Team, a two-boat unit attached to a SEAL platoon. We had the 36ft Medium SEAL Support Craft (MSSC), capable of supporting a platoon, and the Light SEAL Support Craft (LSSC), big enough for a SEAL squad. I was a coxswain on one of the MSSCs; we did insertions and extractions for the SEALs, 'water-borne guard posts'—the usual sort of SEAL support missions. We had our share of fire-fights, just like the SEALs did. Some of the boats got chopped up, some people got hurt.

"A fire fight for a SEAL support craft usually happened at night. It happened extremely fast—green tracers headed toward you, red tracers headed toward them. You shot them up while you tried to exit the area, calling for air and artillery fire support at the same time. They never lasted more than a couple of minutes, at the outside. We used M-60s, .50cal machine guns, the old Mk 18 grenade launcher—and the mini-gun was a *great* ambush breaker! An ambush is broken with a tremendous volume of firepower, combined with a rapid exit from the area. The grenade launcher and the mini-gun were the two greatest ambush breakers in the world, highly recommended for riverine warfare."

The mission for the boats begins about the same time it does for the SEAL platoon, with the receipt of the "warning order." The boat OIC (officer in charge) will do his planning and preparation with the SEALs for his portion of the op, working out the SOPs and coordinating with the team. That will certainly include a "map recon," a study of the chart of the area the boats will transit and the objective area. The fuel tanks get topped off, water, ammunition, a couple of cases of MREs ("Meal, Ready to Eat") are stowed. Do the radios all work? Are the engines reliable? Are the weapons clean and functional?

Those water spouts are outgoing, not incoming rounds, you'll be pleased to know. Special Boat Squadron crew test fire the "ma deuce" M2 .50cal machine gun. Gary Kieffer/Foto Consortium

tions have all rebuilt the bond again. While our primary mission is to support the SEAL platoons, we have an offensive capability on our own; we can do coastal patrol, interdiction, riverine warfare—without SEALs aboard. We support not only SEALs but Army Special Forces and Marine Force Recon."

The senior chief adds, "The SEALs, though, should get the glory; they go all the way on the missions, and they've earned it. We in the SBUs don't mind being in the shadows—that's our tradition in NSW—we are the silent ones.

The old PBRs are about worn out now, but they have a rich combat legacy from the "big war" in Viet Nam. Gary Kieffer/Foto Consortium

"We usually left about sundown, transited to our op area, making false insertions along the way. We dropped off the SEALs and then made a few more false insertions so the enemy never really knew where we left them. Sometimes we just put the guys aboard a sampan, towed them along behind us, and cut them loose to drift ashore while we continued on. We even had a few where the SEALs jumped off the boat and swam in to the bank—but that was a rarity. Most of the time, though, we would just nose in to a beach and let them off. They were really good at that, too—a lot better during Viet Nam than they are now! Back then, you could get a SEAL squad ashore in three to five seconds, but not any more. The urgency of war made for a much more intense operation."

While the SEALs "sneak and peek," the boat will remain in the general vicinity, about a mile away. During Viet Nam the boat provided a necessary service as radio relay station; the squad's PRC-77 didn't have the range to let the team talk to anybody more than a few miles away, depending on terrain. But the boat's powerful radios were another story.

The boats' most important function, though, then and now, is to collect the team when the time comes to leave.

That time can be any time after the insertion. If the team gets into a fight with a bigger unit they will probably want to call for support and extraction. Regardless, sometime before first light, they will move to a pre-determined extraction point (not the same place where they inserted) and climb back on the boats for the trip back.

Coastal Patrol Ships—PC Class

SPECWARCOM's official pride and joy is supposed to be the new Hurricane-class coastal patrol ships; thirteen of the vessels will provide NSW with its own little fleet of warships. It is a very odd vessel, a design not everybody thinks makes sense for the missions SEALs conduct.

First, the fundamentals: the PC ships are 170ft long, 25ft in the beam, draw about 8ft of water under the keel. It will survive Sea State Five (8ft to 12ft waves), cruise at 12 knots, with a dash capability (at tremendous fuel economy penalty) of 35 knots, and a maximum range of 2,000 miles. Thirty-two Special Boat Squadron officers and men crew the vessel. It is supposed to be a long-range, high-endurance patrol vessel, able to stay on station for extended periods.

But it only supports a single SEAL squad—eight men. It is under-gunned, considering its missions, with just a Mk 38 25mm chain gun forward, another Mk 38 aft, pedestals for Stinger missiles, and four mounts for .50cal and 7.62mm machine guns or Mk 19 grenade launch-

ers. It mounts two chaff/decoy dispensers behind the wheel-house to counter the missile threat, but many modern missiles can now counter the chaff and decoys.

"Most of us don't like them," one anonymous boat driver reports. "They are big enough to be a good target for a missile. You don't shoot a missile at a small rubber boat, but this thing is a *target*. And, for its size, it is vastly under-armed. It doesn't have the capability to go up against a third-world navy combatant craft. The Mk 38 is a good gun, until it is time to reload—that takes forever! And here's a 170ft ship that only supports eight SEALs—that's ridiculous."

The first real-world use of the PC was in Haitian waters in 1994—and one managed to run aground.

Mk III Patrol Boat

One of the primary lessons learned by the Navy's web-footed warriors in the slime of the Mekong Delta was the importance of suitable patrol boats to support the SEAL mission. The Mk III Sea Spectre Patrol Boat is a 65ft, aluminum-hulled workhorse, propelled by a trio of

Now here's a rare picture of a 30ft RIB underway; normally this is done in the middle of the night, with winds gusting to 20 knots and seas to 8ft and a boat load of SEALs hanging on for dear life. Robert Genat/Zone Five Photo

Here's a High-Speed Boat (HSB) showing off for the crowd. The HSB was another dubious hull when it was introduced during the 1980s, but it got a workout and performed well in the Persian Gulf in operations against Iraq. It is essentially an off-shore ocean racer with machine guns and tactical radios. The maintenance required is tremendous. But when a boat lets you do missions that need doing and that can't be done otherwise, the maintenance hours become less important. Robert Genat/Zone Five Photo

diesel engines to a maximum speed of about 25 knots. It was intended to be a highly potent gun platform, ready and able to duke it out with quite a few bad guys. Mk IIIs use a modular approach to weapons, selected for each mission—two .50cal machine guns, grenade launchers, M-60s—and a chip-on-the-shoulder attitude that the enemy quickly learned to respect.

The Mk III has been in on all the major campaigns of the past couple of decades—Grenada, Lebanon, and the Persian Gulf during Ernest Will and Desert Storm.

High Speed Boat

The HSBs are "wave-skippers," the boat crews say, and very maintenance-intensive. They are essentially off-shore "cigarette" racing boat designs adapted for Navy use, huge engines stuffed into slender, expensive hulls. A four-hour operation will require about eighty hours of maintenance.

But the HSBs earned their keep in the Persian Gulf. They patrolled, inserted SEAL recon swimmers, chased Iraqi boats, and shot up the shoreline and selected targets offshore. They were available to pluck pilots from the water, if needed, and they helped pull of one of the great deceptions of modern military history when two HSBs inserted swimmers along the coast just before Desert Storm kicked off. The swimmers planted explosives and noise-makers along an obvious invasion beach, set the timers, and exfiltrated aboard the HSBs. When the blasts started, the Iraqi defenders prepared for a US Marine Corps assault and called for reinforcements. The little operation by a squad of SEALs and Special Boat Squadron crewmen took about four enemy divisions out of the fight—a lot of bang for the buck!

Rigid-Hull Inflatable Boats

The Rigid-Hull Inflatable boats (called "ribs" and spelled "RIBs") have pretty much taken over the clandestine insertion and extraction mission from the old speedboats like the Sea Fox. The RIB design is a hybrid: the keel portion of the hull is fiberglass while the upper portion of the hull is an inflatable series of cells constructed of a nylon/neoprene combination called Hypalon. The combination provides plenty of cargo capacity, speed potential, and low radar signature, all of which are prime virtues in the SEAL bag of tricks. The Hypalon won't actually deflect bullets, but it is extremely tough and puncture resistant.

The design actually comes from the commercial world where similar boats have been in use for about twenty years. The Coast Guard loves the RIBs and wrings theirs out even harder than SEALs do. Naval Special Warfare and the Special Boat Squadrons use three variations on the concept, in 24ft, 30ft, and 10m (33ft) lengths.

24-Foot RIB

Two 24ft RIBs support one squad of SEALs, one fire team, and their gear in each. They are strong, stable boats able to tolerate Sea-State Five, but it is a cold, wet ride. There is a lot of pounding and you have to be in good physical condition to just ride in one.

The boat will do 25 knots on flat water, powered by a Volvo Penta marine inboard engine; maximum range is 175 nautical miles (nm). It draws only 2ft, so it can get a fire team ashore with nearly dry feet. At 9,300lb it is a bit too heavy to use as a PT training aid (as the smaller CRRC is used at BUD/S). Like the other RIBs, the 24ft version is tricked out with radar, an M-60 machine gun, and radios.

"We aren't SEALs," says one of the Special Boat Squadron crew with a lot of time in the RIBs, "but we have to be in better shape than a sailor aboard ship. Sometimes the seas are so rough that you literally get beaten black and blue. You get cold, numb, and your knees feel like they've turned to jelly. You haven't lived till you've pulled an eight-hour mission on one of these things on a cold, windy night during horrendous weather! But real good ops are done in real bad weather—that's when the sentries on the beach won't be watching out to sea all that much. Being miserable is just part of the program!"

The USS Hurricane, *third ship in the Coastal Patrol class.*
Robert Genat/Zone Five Photo

At anchor not far from Coronado, the 170ft PC is a new and somewhat puzzling sight for SEALs. It brings a new capability to NSW, the option of "forward deployment" of a squad of SEALs to trouble spots around the globe. While many vessels provide patrol functions, and other vessels provide SEAL support, the PC is the first to put both together in the same dedicated hull. It is the first ship (as opposed to boat) designed for NSW. Robert Genat/Zone Five Photo

30-Foot RIB

The 30ft inflatable has the same mission, with more cargo and passenger room. It is a beamy little vessel, 11ft across the gunwales with grab rails for the passengers, who tend to get a wild ride. It tilts the scales at about 15,000lb, partly a result of those big twin diesel engines and the "Jacuzzi" water-jet propulsion system. Top speed is 32 knots, max range is 150 miles. It is the platform of choice for clandestine, over-the-horizon insertions.

10-Meter RIB

The 24ft and 30ft RIBs worked so well that RDT&E staff decided to design and build an even bigger variant of the design, a 10 meter (about 33ft) model. It isn't, as of this writing, working too well. It is supposed to have a 40 knot top speed and a range of 250 nautical miles but the prototypes have been beating themselves to death.

Mk IV Patrol Boat

The Mk IV is a 68ft boat based on the Mk III, but with more powerful engines. Armament includes machines guns, grenade launchers, and a pair of 25mm chain guns. The Mk IV saw action during the Just Cause operation in Panama.

Mk II Patrol Boat

Although this design is about 30 years old, Mk IIs are still in service with the SBUs. It is a 32ft hull with twin .50cal heavy machine guns forward, .30cal machine

guns and grenade launchers aft, and the capability of mounting a 60mm mortar for both direct (line of sight) and indirect fire. The Mk II was a workhorse in the Mekong Delta during the war in Viet Nam, then went on to fight in the Persian Gulf and Panama with SBU-26.

Patrol Boat Light (PBL)

The PBL is a modified Boston Whaler, a 25ft utility boat with a fiberglass hull. The PBL mounts a "Ma Deuce" M2.50cal, a .30cal M60 machine gun, plus the personal weapons of the crew and any SEALs embarked. It is especially valuable for its easy "fly-away" capability; the design saw service in Panama.

MATC

The MATC is a fast river support craft for SEAL platoons. It is a 36ft vessel with a 30knots-plus capability and mounts for seven crew-served weapons.

CRRC

The Combat Rubber Raiding Craft is strictly a SEAL resource, owned and operated by the SEAL teams rather than the Special Boat Squadrons. It is just 15ft long and 6ft wide; empty, it weighs 265lb. You can get eight SEALs aboard with personal gear, but that's pushing it if you are going to operate in the open ocean. Powerplants range from 35hp to 55hp, with an 8-SEAL-

This stern-aspect view of the PC shows the little platform designed for swimmer and RIB launch and recovery. Robert Genat/Zone Five Photo

power paddle option available. With a standard 16gal tank of gas, a light load, and flat seas, you can roam for about 65 nautical miles before the engine quits.

These little boats get a tremendous workout. It is the CRRC that gets stowed in a submarine's SEAL gear locker for lock in/lock out operations; it is often carried inflated on the forecastle of any of the patrol boats, ready to put SEALs over the side for a little excursion.

Index